May 15, 2014, Fort Clatsop Bookstore
Lewis & Clark National Park

D1015257

POMP

The Long, Adventurous Life of Sacagawea's Son

by

Frederick Taylor

authorHOUSE

1663 Liberty Drive, Suite 200
Bloomington, Indiana 47403
(800) 839-8640
www.authorhouse.com

No part of this book may be reproduced, stored in a retrieval system, or transmitted by any means without the written permission of the author.

First published by AuthorHouse 07/09/04

ISBN: 1-4184-4533-9 (e)
ISBN: 1-4184-4534-7 (sc)

Library of Congress Control Number: 2004093802

Printed in the United States of America
Bloomington, Indiana

This book is printed on acid-free paper.

Grateful acknowledgement is made of the following for granting permission to reprint excerpts:

From "Sakakawea - The Bird Woman," by Russell Reid, Copyright 1986, State Historical Society of North Dakota, Bismarck;

From "Letters of the Lewis and Clark Expedition," Second Edition, Volume 2, edited by Donald Jackson, Copyright 1978, University of Illinois Press, Urbana;

From "Sacajawea?–Sakakawea?–Sacagawea?" by Irving W. Anderson, Summer 1975 issue of We Proceeded On, Copyright 2001, the Lewis and Clark Trail Heritage Foundation, Great Falls, Montana.

ACKNOWLEDGMENTS

One of the delights for an amateur biographer in writing a book such as this is the discovery that there are so many people willing to help in finding and sorting out the pertinent research. This particularly is true of the dedicated people at historical societies and university libraries.

Those to whom I am obliged include: Carl Hallberg, American Heritage Center, the University of Wyoming, Laramie; Kristinia Gray Perez and Jason D. Stratman, Missouri Historical Society, St. Louis; Laura Ries, South Dakota State Historical Society, Pierre; Rhonda Brown, State Historical Society of North Dakota, Bismarck; Barbara Dey, Colorado Historical Society, Denver; Russ Taylor, Special Collections, Harold B. Lee Library, Brigham Young University, Provo, Utah; Megan Vandehey, Roger & Julie Baskes Department of Special Collections, The Newberry Library, Chicago; Matt Walker, Idaho State Historical Society, Boise; David H. Wallace, National Archives, Washington, D.C.; the staff of the Malheur County Library, Ontario, Oreg. And special thanks to researchers Cullen Gerst, Berkeley; Coralee Paull, St. Louis; Mary Ann Maxwell, Provo, Utah, and to translator-researchers Gene Wright and Marlis Houghton of Coos Bay, Oregon.

I also want to commend the University of Oklahoma Press and the University of Nebraska Press for their dedication to the literature of the Old West. Their publication of both original journals and reprints of books long out of print have, at reasonable cost, saved many books valuable to historians and western buffs alike from disappearance.

Finally, I'd like to add a note of appreciation for the late historian Grace Raymond Hebard, of whom I am otherwise critical in this book. It was through her efforts seventy-five years ago that the journals of Prince Paul Wilhelm of Wurttemburg were located in Germany, translated and thus saved. Historians of the fur trading days are in her debt because the original manuscripts apparently were destroyed in World War II.

FT

Charleston, Oregon

March, 2004

TO GEORGA

For Her Love and Patience

TABLE OF CONTENTS

PREFACE

Many of the people in this book were illiterate and most of those who weren't didn't spell well by today's standards. Because the information in this book is almost entirely from journals, letters and documents from that period, the spelling within it is exactly that rendered in the original material. There is no effort to correct for spelling, grammar or punctuation.

This may cause a certain amount of confusion to the reader, but can be charming. (And will corrupt your own grammar and spelling). Captain William Clark, for example, was probably the most imaginative speller of the early west, relying heavily on phonetics. "Mockersons" for moccasins and, even finer, "musquetors" for mosquitoes are two of his gems. "Durtey" for dirty is another nice coinnage. And "axcessable" and "secumpherance." The other journalists were nearly as inventive.

The confused spelling particularly affects the names of three of the principal characters in this book: Sacagawea and the Charbonneaus, father and son. Of the latter you will find by Clark, who wasn't bound by consistency, Shabono, Shabounar, Charbonah, Shabowner, Shabonah and Charbono; consistently Charbono by Lewis, and from other writers Charbenau, Charbonet, Charbineaux, Chabeneau, Chabonard. By internal evidence, the names all refer to either Toussaint, the father, or Jean Baptiste, the son, although their given names also sometimes were mangled.

Sacagawea presents a case of her own. For many years there was a lively, if academic, debate over both the spelling of the Indian woman's name and its meaning. Some of that was geographically inspired.

Irving W. Anderson's article in the summer, 1975 issue of *"We Proceeded On"* was entitled "Sacajawea?—Sakakawea?—Sacagawea?," neatly summing up the problem.

"With respect to her name," he wrote, "it is found spelled fourteen times total, by Lewis and Clark, and once by Sergeant John Ordway in the explorers' original manuscript journals, primary documentary sources. Although their flair for inspired spelling created some interesting variations, in every instance, including three additional spellings on Clark's maps, all three of the journalists who attempted to write it were consistent in the use of a "g" in the third syllable. Lewis gave not only his rendition of the spelling of her name but also its meaning. His journal entry for May 20, 1805, reads: "a handsome river of about fifty yards in width discharged itself into the shell river on the Star[boar]d or upper side; this stream we called Sah-ca-gah-we-ah or bird woman's River, after our interpreter the Snake woman."

Anderson noted that the U.S. Geographic Names Board, the National Parks Service and the National Geographic Society, among others, have adopted the Sacagawea spelling. Although she was a Shoshone, her name is traced to the Hidatsa Indian tribe, among whom she lived for most of her life. He said her name derived from two Hidatsa Indian words: sacaga, meaning bird, and wea, meaning woman, and is pronounced with a hard "g." Clark said that in taking Indian vocabularies "great object was to make every letter sound."

People wanting to emphasize her Shoshone heritage claim her as Sacajawea, the form of her name with which many of us grew up. This spelling complicates matters; it means "boat launcher," or "boat pusher" in Shoshone. But Lewis and Clark, in naming the river, certainly understood her name to mean bird woman.

The "j" spelling was used, for no apparent reason—Anderson said the only reason was "editorial prerogative"—in the publication "History of The Expedition Under the Command of Captains Lewis and Clark," edited by Nicholas Biddle, of the Philadelphia Biddles. He took on the job, at the request of President Jefferson after the death in 1809 of Meriwether Lewis, who was supposed to have prepared them but continually postponed the chore. Even then publication faced difficulties; the original printer went bankrupt.

So it wasn't until 1814 that an account of the great exploration, which ended in 1806, finally was published from their journals. (Patrick Gass, a member of the company, published his own account in 1807, which was a great success; at least six editions were printed, including three in Europe. But Gass apparently didn't get much out of this success, reportedly only receiving one hundred copies.)

And Biddle's work wasn't satisfactory. He wrote a narrative, working from the captains' longhand entries, plus interviews with Clark, corrected spelling and grammar, and abridged many daily entries. He spelled her name Sacajawea.

In 1893 a highly edited version of the journals was published by Elliott Coues. He noted that the Indian woman's name "usually is spelled Sacajawea."

Finally, in 1904, 98 years after the journey was completed, Reuben Gold Thwaites published, in eight volumes, the original journals verbatim. This book follows the Thwaites edition.

Anderson said the Sakakawea spelling was promoted by Hidatsa advocates in North Dakota. This spelling, he said, was independently constructed from two Hidatsa Indian words found in a dictionary titled: "Ethnography and Philoloqy of the Hidatsa Indians," published by the Govenment Printing Office in 1877, compiled by U.S. Army Surgeon Dr. Washington Matthews 65 years after her death. And so, in North Dakota today, there is a Lake Sakakawea, created by the Garrison dam on the Missouri, and on the capitol grounds in Bismarck a monument to her spelled the same way. And there's one in South Dakota, too.

This book, when in the writer's voice, goes with Sacagawea. When it uses quotation, it follows *that* writer's use. Sometimes this means, in the course of a single sentence, the Indian heroine's name is spelled two different ways.

A final point: The period this book covers was before the natives became the recently accepted Native Americans. So Indians are called Indians here. Indian women are called squaws, those of mixed races are called half breeds.

1

THE ADVENTURE BEGINS

On May 14, 1804, the Lewis and Clark Expedition pushed off from its camp at Riviere du Bois, on the American east bank of the Mississippi, directly opposite the mouth of the Missouri. The party was in a twenty-two-oar keelboat, fifty feet long, drawing three feet of water and carrying one square sail; a deck of ten feet in the bow and stern formed a forecastle and cabin, and the middle was covered by lockers, with lids that could be raised to provide protection in case of attack. There also were two piroques, or flatbottomed open boats, one of six and the other of seven oars, built for use in shallow water.

On November 3, sixteen hundred miles up the Missouri, one hundred sixty-five days after it had pushed off, the expedition halted and began building its quarters for the winter, Fort Mandan.

On November 11, Clark reported, "two Squars of the Rock mountains, purchased from the Indians by a frenchman came down."

One of them was Sacagawea, who was pregnant.

In January, 1803, President Thomas Jefferson had sent a secret message to Congress in which he explained the financial advantages of fur trade with the Indians and asked for an appropriation of $2,500 for "the purpose of extending the external commerce of the United States." He said he had in mind an expedition that would gather information about the Indians, including the trading prospects, and almost in passing allowed that it was possible it might explore "even to the Western ocean," and might "incidenteally advance the geographical knowledge of our own continent..."

This was a project in which Jefferson had long been interested. In 1783, when he was in Congress, he wrote to the most celebrated Westerner, George Rogers Clark, asking whether he would lead an expedition to the west if the money could be raised to finance it.

The British, Jefferson said, had raised a large sum "for exploring the country from the Mississippi to California," and while the ostensible reason was "only to promote knoledge," he was "afraid that they have thoughts of colonizing into that quarter."

The money for Clark wasn't raised. So, 20 years later, Jefferson as president got it.

The man Jefferson picked to lead the expedition was Meriwether Lewis, lately a captain of infantry in the U.S. Army but for the past two years his personal secretary. And the man *Lewis* picked to help him was William Clark, George Rogers Clark's young brother, who had been Lewis's commanding officer in the army for a few months eight years earlier. Lewis offered Clark, who had been a lieutenant when he resigned the army in 1796, a captaincy. The War Department, in one of the fits of pettiness not unknown in Washington today, refused to approve the promotion. Clark said later, "My feelings on this Occasion was as might be expected." But never mind. The troops were not to be told and Clark was always

2

known to the expedition's members as captain and so signed his official papers. Both men were frontiersmen, experienced woodsmen and rivermen. But the slight continued to rankle. Three weeks after the expedition made its triumphant return to St. Louis, Clark resigned his commission in the army.

Although in his secret message to Congress Jefferson barely alluded to it, he had much more that mere commerce in mind, and Lewis, who had been working for him for two years, knew it. The goal: Beat the British overland to the Pacific and thus stake a claim over the huge territory for the U.S. But the destination and ultimate purpose of the expedition were to be disguised. "The idea that you are going to explore the Missisipi has been generally given out: it satisfies public curiousity, and masks sufficiently the real destination," Jefferson wrote Lewis.

It wasn't the last time a president would mislead Congress about his goals.

The project started off small enough. The Emperor Napoleon had recently compelled the Spanish to turn over what was known as Louisiana to the French. And they were threatening to bar Americans from the Mississippi River, which was becoming an American waterway. Jefferson wanted to buy New Orleans, which controlled the mouth of the great river, to prevent that happening.

So negotiations began desultorily, toward that end. Then, suddenly and as a great shock to the American negotiators, Napolean's foreign minister casually asked, How much would the United States pay for *all* of Louisiana?

Even though the ministers, Robert Livingston and James Monroe, had been instructed to offer $2,000,000 only for New Orleans, the deal was quickly struck. A treaty dated April 30, 1803 clinched it: $15,000,000 for the whole place.

The United States had just doubled in size.

And there still was that vast area west of the Rocky Mountains not yet claimed with authority by anyone.

Preparations for the Lewis and Clark Expedition, formally known as the Corps of Discovery, had already been underway before the negotiations were completed. The two leaders kept busy recruiting members—who would be sworn into the army—training them, buying equipment and supplies, including 21 bales of presents for the Indians, and building boats.

Finally ready, the expedition headed upstream, to what would be its quarters for the winter of 1804-1805.

On February 11, 1805, at the Mandan Indian villages, Captain William Clark recorded the following in his diary:

"about five Oclock this evening one of the wives of Charbono was delivered of a fine boy. it is worthy to remark that this was the first child which this woman had boarn, and as is common in such cases her labour was tedious and the pain violent; Mr. Jessome informed me that he had frequently administered a small portion of the rattle of the rattle-snake, which he assured me had never failed to produce the desired effect, that of hastening the birth of the child; having the rattle of a snake by me I gave it to him and he administered two rings of it to the woman broken in small pieces with the fingers and added to a small quantity of water. Whether this medicine was truly the cause or not I shall not undertake to determine, but I was informed that she had not taken it more than ten minutes before she brought forth perhaps this remedy may be worth of future experiments, but I confess I want faith as to it's efficacy."

The "wife of Charbono" was, of course, Sacagawea, who was to become one of the most famous women, white or Indian, in U.S. history. And the fine boy was Jean Baptiste Charbonneau, birth weight unknown. He was the only member of the great Lewis and Clark Expedition to the Pacific Ocean who rode the whole way, mostly on his mother's back. He went on to lead an adventuresome life that took him to St. Louis and an education at Clark's expense, to six years in Europe as the guest and ward of a German prince, to years in the mountain west as a fur trapper, interpreter and guide, back to the Pacific as a guide for a battalion of Mormon soldiers, a short tour as the alcalde, or justice of the peace, of a Spanish mission, to the California gold fields after the 1848 discovery there and then, 61 years after his birth at Fort Mandan, to death in a remote corner of Oregon.

That both Sacagawea and Baptiste even survived their 3,900-mile trip is extraordinary. They, with the other thirty-one members of the expedition, battled rain, snow and floods, and several times nearly starved. On top of that, both became seriously ill and, of course, the illness of the mother threatened the life of the infant, who was nursing.

But survive they did.

Sacagawea, after Lewis and Clark the most noted member of the expedition, was born about 1788, near what today is Salmon, in eastern Idaho, a member of the Snake, or Shoshone, tribe. When she was about ten, the band traveled east to the Three Forks, where three rivers join to form the headwaters of the Missouri River. There the band was attacked by Minnetaree Indians, she later told Lewis, and killed four men, four women, a number of boys and made prisoners of all the females and four boys. Sacagawea was captured in the middle of the river as she was trying to make her escape.

Sacagawea was a slave of the Minnetarees for several years and then won or purchased by Toussaint Charbonneau, a French Canadian trapper, fur trader and interpreter who had been living with them for five years or more; she was ten or twelve at the time. Charbonneau also acquired another young Shoshone girl about then.

Squaws were treated badly in the Indian world and squaw captives even worse, "just livestock," one historian says of their situation. And beasts of burden. The

5

Journals report that on a dangerously steep path after the expedition reached the coast, Clark saw the pack a squaw was carrying slip from her back and she grabbed a bush to keep from going over the side. Clark rushed to help and found the load "almost as much as he could lift, and above one hundred pounds in weight."

Toussaint Charbonneau, born in Montreal about 1759, worked for a time as a trader for the Northwest Company on the Assiniboine River of Canada. The trader John MacDonnell recorded one of his adventures. An old squaw caught Charbonneau "in the act of committing a Rape upon her Daughter," and administered a canoe awl so vigorously on him that he could hardly get back to his canoe, "a fate he highly deserved for his brutality."

When Lewis and Clark reached the Mandan Indian country in late October of 1804, north of what today is Bismarck, North Dakota, Charbonneau was living in a nearby Minnetaree village. Sacagawea was his "wife," although it is unlikely a wedding ceremony had been performed. She was no more than seventeen, and probably younger, when her son was born. Charbonneau was forty-six. He had a taste for young Indian women into his old age.

Neither Lewis nor Clark had much regard for Charbonneau. In March they'd offered him a job as a translator on the expedition but he said he'd only take it if he didn't have to stand guard and if "miffed with any man," he could leave whenever he wanted.

They said no thanks. Five days later Charbonneau reapplied for the job, saying that he was sorry "for the foolish part he had acted" and would do whatever the captains asked if they'd take him. They realized that Charbonneau together with Sacagawea would be a valuable team. He could interpret as long as they were among the river Indians and Sacagawea's knowledge of Shoshone would greatly help when they reached the Rocky Mountain Indians.

So Charbonneau hired on, bringing along the young Indian woman, and, of course, her child.

Talking with the Indians always presented a problem; sign language could only go so far. One approach was described by Charles MacKenzie, a British trader from Canada, who paid a call on the captains: "Sacagawea spoke a little Hidatsa [Minnetaree]," he wrote, "in which she had to converse with her husband, who was Canadian and did not understand English. A mulatto [Rene Jessaume, a trader living with the Minnetarees], who spoke bad French and worse English, served as interpreter to the Captains, so that a single word to be understood by the party required to pass from the natives to the woman, from the woman to the husband, from the husband to the mulatto, from the mulatto to the captains." Furthermore, Charbonneau and Jessaume argued about the meaning of every French word they used.

If all else failed, they could resort to sign language. Lewis said that George Druillard, a French-Canadian hired as an interpreter for the expedition, "understood perfectly the common language of jesticulation or signs which seem to be universaly understood by all the Nations we have yet seen. it is true that this language is imperfect and liable to error but is much less so than would be expected. the strong parts of the ideas are seldom mistaken."

All that made for long conferences.

The expedition spent a relatively comfortable winter with the Mandans, building a fort, called Fort Mandan, that enclosed cabins with fireplaces, which kept them warm despite the bitter cold. One day in December the temperature hit 42 degrees below zero. There was plenty of work to keep busy. They built a big smokehouse, twenty-four by fourteen feet, and on one hunting trip the party brought in thirty-two deer, twelve elk and a buffalo. So there was enough food most of the time. And celebrations at Christmas and New Years's, with big meals, singing and dancing, music provided by Private Peter Cruzatte, who had brought his fiddle on the trek, and modest drinking. Sacagawea watched the Christmas celebration, along with Charbonneau's other Snake squaw.

And there were agreeable Indian women, with the predictable results: Some of the men came down with venereal diseases. Clark, years later, commented that they "were the handsomest women in the world."

Even before the expedition reached the Mandan villages, women were available. In mid-October the travelers stopped at a big village of Arikaras, called Rickeres by Clark. He noted "a curious custom with the Souix as well as the rickeres is to give handsom squars to those whome they wish to Show some acknowledgements to. The Seauex we got clare of without taking their squars, they followed us with Squars two days. The Richores we put off dureing the time we were at the Towns but 2 [*hansom young*] Squars were Sent by a man to follow us, they came up this evening, and pursisted in their civilities."

The next day, at another Arikara camp, he reported, "Those people are much pleased with my black Servent." York was the first black man the Indians had ever seen. "Their womin verry fond of carressing our men &c."

Western legend is that there were highly visible descendants of York from one end of the trail to the other.

One factor that made the Mandan girls attractive to the whites was that many of them were light colored. This light color, word of which had been spread down river by visiting trappers and traders for years, gave strength to the legend of a tribe of "white Indians," descendants of Welsh explorers. The story, which was printed in a pamphlet in 1583 in England, said that a Welsh prince named Madoc had discovered America in 1170, liked what he saw, went back to Wales and gathered up a crowd of followers, who then started colonies, depending upon who was telling the story, in Virginia, or Florida, Panama, Newfoundland, or the West

Indies, then prospered or died, or moved west, where they intermarried with the natives. Then the stories merged; the consensus was that the Mandan Indians were, in fact, the Welsh Indians, or at least their descendants.

President Jefferson was interested in the Welsh Indians. In 1804, as the expedition was getting organized, he wrote Lewis, enclosing a translation of a dispatch, originally written in Spanish, by a man named John Evans, a Welshman working for the Spanish government. He was map making for the Spanish, Jefferson said, "but whose original object I believe had been to go in search of the Welsh Indians, said to be up the Missouri." He told Lewis to keep an eye out for them.

Lewis and Clark decided the Mandans weren't Welsh. Their light color probably was the result of the visits over many years by Canadian trappers. However, the captains didn't give up their effort to find them. Private Joseph Whitehouse, in his journal of the expedition, reported on another possibility when the company was far to the west, among the Flathead Indians. "these Savages has the Strangest language of any we have ever Seen," he wrote. "we take these Savages to be the Welch Indians if their be any Such from the Language. So Capt. Lewis took down the names of everry thing in their Language, in order that it may be found out whether they are or whether they Sprang or origenated first from the welch or not."

Another disappointment; they weren't.

The legend of the Welsh Indians lasted a long time. The painter George Catlin became convinced upon visiting the Mandans in 1832 they were the ones. He noted they used small round boats much like Welsh coracles and some of their words sounded like the words he had heard among Welsh-speaking miners in the Pennsylvania coal country. He later changed his mind.

One of the finest of the stories about the white Indians was heard in the Southwest in the 1840s. Rufus Sage wrote at length about them in his book *Rocky Mountain*

Life. Sage was visiting Fort Unitah in the foothills of the Unitah Mountains when a company that had been trapping on the Gila River pulled in.They reported they'd spent four weeks in Sonora, Mexico, with a white-skinned tribe of about eight hundred people called "the Munchies." They lived in spacious apartments carved out of the cliffsides, farmed and raised cattle, sheep and horses, and made butter and cheese. "Their features correspond with those of Europeans, though with a complexion, perhaps, somewhat fairer, and a form equally if not more graceful," Sage wrote. After pondering the matter, he decided the Munchies probably were the descendants of "some colony of ancient Romans." They were never seen by anyone else. Brigham Young expected to run into the Welsh Indians in Utah. He didn't.

On April 7 the expedition, without solving the puzzle of the Welsh Indians, left its winter quarters and started upriver, in six small canoes and two perogues. The keelboat, too large to be used above the Indian villages, was sent back to St. Louis.

Two days later, Sacagawea began to show her value to the expedition. Lewis reported that when the flotilla had stopped for dinner, she "busied herself in serching for wild artichokes" which she found by digging with a sharp stick, and got "a good quantity." It was the first of her many forays for roots and berries.

In May, she proved her worth again. Charbonneau was at the helm of a perogue under sail when a vicious squall hit it, laying it on its side, and only the awning at the stern, under which Sacagawea and Baptiste rested, prevented the boat from turning "topsaturva," as Lewis put it. The boat filled within an inch of the gunnels and Charbonneau, who couldn't swim, and was "perhaps the most timid waterman in the world," was "crying to his god for mercy." He hadn't "recollected the rudder, nor could the repeated orders of the Bowsman, Cruzat, bring him to her recollection until he threatened to shoot him instantly if he did not take hold of the rudder, and do his duty."

Charbonneau finally did, two men started bailing with kettles and the others rowed the boat ashore.

This upset was potentially catastrophic. Two others aboard couldn't swim, (and if Sacagawea could, she had the baby to tend), the waves were running high and the shore was three hundred yards away. If the boat had gone down, they surely would have drowned.

Nearly as serious was that the perogue was loaded with the expedition's scientific instruments, medicines, books and much of the merchandise for trade with the Indians. A lot went over the side.

Sacagawea cooly retrieved it. Commented Lewis about her behavior: "The Indian woman to whom I ascribe equal fortitude and resolution, with any person on board at the time of the accedent, caught and preserved most of the light articles which were washed overboard."

The affair was traumatic enough that that evening "we thought it a proper occasion to console ourselves and cheer up the sperits of our men and accordingly took a drink of grog and gave each man a gill of sperits."

No record whether Sacagawea got a gill.

In early June Sacagawea became very sick. She may have been ill earlier. In late January Clark recorded that "a Missunderstanding took place between the two inturpeters on account of their squars." One of Charbonneau's squaws was ill, he wrote, and so he ordered that his servant give her "froot Stewed" and tea, which caused the misunderstanding. The interpreters were Jessaume and Charbonneau, and the latter's sick squaw may have been Sacagawea, which wouldn't be surprising since she was nine months pregnant at the time. Since he had two wives, the identity of the sick one isn't certain, but some historians have assumed it was Sacagawea.

This latest illness was serious. For the next two weeks the journal entries of both Lewis and Clark almost daily reported her condition and the treatment they applied. It was the best known to them, but it is a wonder she survived.

Clark noted, on June 10, that "Sahcahgagwea our Indian woman was verry sick. I blead her." He did that the next day also, the standard treatment at the time. The next day she was so sick that Clark moved her into the stern of the perogue under the awning there, where it was cool. The following day he reported that she had been complaining all night and she was "excessivly bad this morning. her case is somewhat dangerous."

Two days later Lewis, who had been scouting upriver, where he reached the Great Falls of the Missouri, returned to camp "and found the Indian woman extremely ill and much reduced by her indisposition. this gave me some concern as well for the poor object herself, then with a young child in her arms, as from consideration of her being our only dependence for a friendly negociation with the Snake Indians on whom we depend for horses to assist us in our portage from the Missouri to the Columbia river..."

Lewis set to work with his own treatment. Earlier the expedition had discovered a sulphur spring below the camp, and he gave her a large drink from that. "I found that the two dozes of barks and opium which I had given her since my arrival had produced an alteration in her pulse for the better; they were now much fuller and more regular...when I first came down I found that her pulse was scarecely perceptible, very quick frequently irregular and attended with strong nervous symptons, that of twitching of the fingers and leaders of the arm; now the pulse had become regular much fuller and a gentle perspiration had taken place; the nervous symptoms have also in great measure abated, and she feels herself much freer from pain, she complains principally of the lower region of the abdomen, I therefore continued the cataplasms of bark and laudnumn which I had previously used..."

While it isn't known what kind of bark Lewis used, he was familiar with barks and herbs as medicine. His mother, in Virginia, was famous for treating sick neighbors with concoctions of them.

Then Lewis made a diagnosis: "I believe her disorder originated principally from an obstruction of the mensis in consequence of taking could [cold]."

That same day Clark reported that "the Indian woman very bad & will take no medisin what ever, untill her husband finding her out of her sences, easily provailed on her to take medison." He added, without explanation, "if she dies it will be the fault of her husband as I am now convinced..."

The next day Lewis noted that Sacagawea was much better, free of pain, fever down, pulse regular. And hungry. She "eats as heartily as I am willing to permit her of boiled buffaloe well seasoned with pepper and salt and rich soope of the same meat."

He continued the home-brew medicine the following day except he added "one doze of 15 drops of the oil of vitriol." She walked out for the first time since the company arrived at this camp.

Then, relapse. Sacagawea was so much better on the morning of June 19 that "she walked out and gathered a considerable quantity of the white apples of which she eats so heartily in their raw state, together with a considerable quantity of dryed fish without my knowledge that she complained very much and her fever again returned.

"I rebuked Sharbono severly for suffering her to indulge herself with such food he being privy to it and having been previously told what she must only eat. I now gave her broken dozes of diluted nitre untill it produced perspiration and at 10 p.m. 30 drops of laudnum which gave her a tolerable nights rest..."

That treatment apparently did the trick.The next day she was up, "walking about and fishing." On June 24, two weeks after she was stricken, Lewis records "the Indian woman is now perfectly recovered."

What caused Sacagawea's illness? Dr. Drake W. Will, in a 1971 monograph "The Medical and Surgical Practices of the Lewis and Clark Expedition," says her illness was due to chronic pelvic inflammatory disease. Dr. Eldon G. Chuinard of Portland, a professor at the University of Oregon's Medical School, (now Oregon Health Sciences University) in 1979 published "Only One Man Died," a review of the medical aspects of the expedition, including the variety of treatments that Lewis and Clark used on its members and Indians alike. Commenting about Will's diagnosis, he says that "her history as a captive-slave of the diseased and licentious Hidatsa lends probability to this diagnosis; if so it probably was gonorrheal in nature."

Hidatsa was another name for the Minnetarees, and to further complicate the situation, the gesture that identified them in sign language was read as Gros Ventres by the French and thus Big Bellies by the British.

Late in June occured another near disaster that, except for the quick action of Clark, would have cost the lives of Sacagawea and Baptiste.

Clark decided to walk overland to the Great Falls of the Missouri, which the expedition had been slowly approaching for days and could hear in the distance. He took with him his servant, the black slave York, another man and Charbonneau, Sacagawea and, on her back, Baptiste. He spotted a black cloud that threatened immediate rain and looked for a place of shelter. Not far above the falls, he spotted a deep ravine with some sheltering rocks and the party took cover there.

Let Clark tell the rest: "the first shower was moderate accompanied by violent wind, the effects of which we did not feel, soon after a torrent of rain and hail fell more violent than ever I saw before, the rain fell like one voley of water falling from the heavens and gave us time only to get out of the way of a torrent of water which was Poreing down the hill in[to] the River with emence force tareing everything before takeing with it large rocks & mud, I took my gun & shot pouch in my left hand, and with the right scrambled up the hill pushing the Interpreters wife (who had her child in her arms) before me, the Interpreter himself makeing attempts to pull up his wife by the hand much scared and nearly without motion we at length reached the top of the hill safe where I found my servent in serch of us greatly agitated, for our wellfar. before I got out of the bottom of the reveen which was a flat dry rock when I entered it, the water was up to my waste & wt my watch, I scercely got out before it raised 10 feet deep with a torrent which [was] turrouble to behold, and by the time I reached the top of the hill at least 15 feet water..."

Clark brought the party back to camp at a run. Baptiste's clothes were all lost, Sacagawea was wet and cold, and the captain, mindful that she'd just recovered from a serious illness, "was fearfull of a relaps." So this time the whole party, including Sacagawea, got "a little spirits" to ward off the chill.

The expedition proceeded under awful conditions. Much of the equipment was buried, to be picked up on the return trip. The two pirogues were hidden. The canoes were manhandled up the river over a rocky bottom while the troops had to look out for grizzly bears, which the journals often call white or yellow bears because of their coloring. They'd been wary of the huge bears since early May when Lewis had an experience that alarmed him. Earlier, after killing a small one—a three-hundred-pound cub—he rather dismissively commented that while they may frighten the Indians, who were armed only with bows and arrows, "in the hands of skillfull riflemen they are by no means as formidable or dangerous as they have been represented." He soon changed his mind. On May 5 Clark went out with George Drouillard and killed one "which we found verry hard to kill we Shot ten Balls into him before we killed him & 5 of those Balls through his lights." Lewis added that after the bear, which weighed five hundred or six hundred pounds, had been shot ten times it swam more than half way across the river to a sandbar and took twenty minutes to die. It measured eight feet seven and a half inches from nose to the ends of its rear feet. The next day he commented dryly that having seen how hard it is to kill one, "I find that the curioussity of our party is pretty well satisfyed with rispect to this anamal." Still later, after another difficult kill, he added another caveat: "these bears being so hard to die reather intimedates us all; I must confess that I do not like the gentlemen and had reather fight two Indians than one bear."

And there were rattlesnakes. Clark and Sacagawea narrowly escaped being bitten; so did Lewis. One soldier was bitten, although not seriously. One after another the men got sick, as Sacagawea already had. Their feet were cut and bruised by the rocks as they dragged the canoes up the river and then when loaded on rough wooden carts, prickly pear spine punctured their moccasins. Clark reported pulling seventeen of the needles out of his feet one night. John Ordway wrote that "One pair of good mockinsons will not last more than about 2 days." Swarms of mosquitoes plagued them. Working nearly naked in the June heat, the party was struck by a sudden hailstorm; one piece weighed three ounces and was seven inches in circumference.One man was knocked down three times, others were bleeding.

Lewis made a bowl of punch with the largest hailstone when the storm ended.

The expedition took a month to go the eighteen miles around the falls, not the day or so that had been anticipated.

The captains were becoming anxious about the absence of Indians. They'd seen none since leaving the Mandans. And if there were no Indians there would be no horses. No horses and, Lewis said, "without horses we shall be obligated to leave a great part of our stores, of which, it appears to me that we have a stock sufficiently small for the length of the voyage ahead."

On July 22 Sacagawea made a discovery that helped create the legend that she was the "guide" of the Lewis and Clark expedition across the continent: at the noonday halt she suddenly recognized the country through which they were passing. This was the river on which her band of Shoshones lived and the Three Forks of the Missouri were just ahead. But as a guide, she wasn't much help after that. When they got to the forks, she didn't know which to take, nor how to find a pass that would lead over the mountains. A few days later she told the captains they were camped on the exact spot where her band had camped when the Minnetarees raided them and she showed them the place where Shosone had hidden and where she was captured. She was "recognizing," not guiding.

Lewis, in his journal, made what turned out to be a surprisingly bad judgment: "Sah-cah-gar-we-ah o[u]r Indian woman was one of the female prisoners taken at that time; tho' I cannot discover that she shews any immotion of sorrow in recollecting this event, or of joy in being restored to her native country; if she has enough to eat and a few trinkets to wear I believe she would be perfectly content anywhere."

Lewis finally found the Snake Indians. And there soon occurred one of the dramatic moments of the expedition.

Biddle's edition of the journals goes into detail:

"On setting out at seven o'clock, Captain Clarke with Charboneau and his wife walked on shore, but they had not gone more than a mile before Clarke saw Sacajawea, who was with her husband a hundred yards ahead, began to dance and show every mark of the most extravagant joy, turning round him and pointing to several Indians, whom he now saw advancing on horseback, sucking her fingers at the same time to indicate they were of her native tribe...

17

"We soon drew near to the camp, and just as we approached it a woman made her way through the crowd towards Sacajawea, and recognizing each other, they embraced with the most tender affection. The meeting of these two young women had in it something peculiarly touching, not only in the ardent manner in which their feelings were expressed, but from the real interest of their situation. They had been companions in childhood, in the war with the Minnetarees they had both been taken prisoners in the same battle, they had shared and softened the rigours of their captivity, till one of them had escaped from the Minnetarees, with scarce hope of ever seeing her friend relieved from the hands of her enemies."

As if that implausible meeting wasn't enough there was another. That evening the Indians and the explorers met in council, seated in a circle. The usual opening ceremonies went on; the peace pipe was passed.

"After this the conference was to be opened, and glad of an opportunity to converse more intelligibly, Sacagajawea was sent for; she came into the tent, sat down and was beginning to interpret, when in the person of Cameahwait [the Snake chief] she recognized her brother: She instantly jumped up, and ran and embraced him, throwing her blanket over him and weeping profusely: The chief was himself moved, though not in the same degree. After some conversation between them she resumed her seat, and attempted to interpret for us, but her new situation seemed to overpower her, and she was frequently interrupted by her tears."

So, contrary to Lewis's initial opinion, the Indian woman did show "immotion."

It should be noted that Biddle, although he spent a week interviewing Clark in writing his narrative of the expedition, consistently misspelled his name. He wasn't the only one. President Jefferson in a document spelled it both Clarke and Clark. The misspelling went on for decades. It wasn't until Historian Elliott Coues tracked down Clark family records in 1892 that it was established the family never added the "e."

There was a sad footnote to the meeting of Sacagawea and her brother. When it was over she learned that all of her family were dead, except for two brothers, one of whom was absent, and a small son of her eldest sister. Following Indian custom, Sacagawea immediately adopted the boy.

The family reunion had a slight complication. Snakes often betrothed their daughters before puberty. When they reached thirteen or fourteen they were sent to their men. Sacagawea had been betrothed—before her capture by the Minnetarees and later sale to Charbonneau—to a warrior twice her age, who now claimed her. But he didn't want her after he learned she'd had a child.

Sacagawea soon performed another important service to the expedition. Cameahwait had promised horses and guides to help the company cross the mountains to what they thought would be the headwaters of the Columbia about a day's march away—a very bad estimate as it turned out. Sacagawea learned that the Indian chief had told his warriors that the next day they would head downriver to hunt buffalo. She told her husband, who didn't get around to telling Lewis until dinner. Lewis was understandably angry at that delay and "could not forbear speaking to him with some degree of asperity on this occasion."

After a lecture from Lewis, the Indian chief agreed to call off the hunt and provide the needed horses. Charbonneau, with trading goods supplied by the captains, even bought a horse for Sacagawea and Baptiste to ride.

Interestingly, Sacagawea probably could have stopped right there. She was home, after all, with what remained of her family, and with her native tribe. She had done the job for which she had been brought, translating the Snakes. But for whatever reason, she continued the trek.

Baptiste rode on his mother's back in a cradleboard, an early version of the back pack. He probably wore disposable diapers, although the journals don't report that; the usual sanitary arrangement for papooses was an animal skin outer cover, with moss or grass stuffed inside.

As the party moved up the mountains, there occurred one of those little incidents that told a lot about both Indians and whites. Lewis observed that one of the Indian women who was leading pack horses had stopped about a mile back and sent the horses on. He asked Cameahwait why, and the chief casually said she'd stopped to have a baby and would be along soon. "In about an hour the woman arrived with her newborn babe," Lewis wrote, "and passed us on her way to the camp apparently as well as she ever was." Then he made a comment that is nonsensical on its face, but was believed, obviously by him, but also others. After observing that Indian women seem to give birth very easily, which he called a gift of nature, he commented, "I have been several times informed by those who were conversant with the fact, that the Indian women who are pregnant by whitemen experience more difficulty in childbirth than when pregnant by an Indian."

2

TO THE PACIFIC AND BACK

The party was traveling over high, rugged mountains, guided by an old Indian the captains called Toby, toward the Continental Divide. It snowed. The company crossed the divide and headed down into the Bitterroot Valley, "over emence hills and Some of the worst roade that ever horses passed our horses frequently fell," Clark wrote. Finally they met a band of Salish Indians, which the captains called Flatheads, although they didn't deform their heads as Indians on the coast sometimes did. These were the Indians that Whitehouse thought might be Welsh. They were friendly and Clark bought eleven more horses. They proceeded on; the terrain was terrible, the mountains steeper and more rugged than before. It snowed. They ran low on food, killing a colt and then resorting to "portable soup," an army experimental ration that nobody liked, (a forerunner that continues to this day of experimental army rations that nobody likes), a coyote, even a crow. Clark said "I have been wet and as cold in every part as I ever was in my life, indeed I was at one time fearfull my feet would freeze in the thin Mockirsons which I wore."

More than a month after they left the Snakes, they met the Nez Perces, who supplied the company with dried salmon and camas root. Nearly the whole company got sick, primarily with dysentery.

"Capt. Lewis scercely able to ride on a jentle horse which was furnished by the Chief," Clark wrote. "Several men So unwell that they were Compelled to lie on the Side of the road for Some time others obliged to be put on horses."

There is a legend among the Nez Perce that the expedition nearly met its end right there. The company was virtually helpless with dysentery. It also was well armed, and the Nez Perce weren't. So the whites were tempting targets, with weapons almost for the taking. But, the story says, an old Indian woman saved them. Years earlier she had been captured by the Blackfeet, taken to Canada and sold to a white, who treated her well. Somehow she got back home and when the expedition showed up she said, "These are the people who helped me. Do them no hurt."

The Nez Perce didn't, instead saving the company from starvation.

The company had arrived on the Clearwater River, where it could resume travel by canoe, which the men who were able to work began building. This was Canoe Camp, about five miles west of today's Orofino, Idaho. On October 7, the expedition was afloat again, in four large and one small canoes.

The trip down the Clearwater, and then on the Snake River after the Clearwater joined it at today's Lewiston, Idaho, was a lot easier than the climb up and down the Bitterroots, but not without serious hazards. The dugout canoes were unwieldy. They leaked, smashed into rocks, turned over, damaged supplies, frightened the passengers. Toby, the Indian guide, had enough of that and decamped without a farewell and without collecting his pay.

The corps passed many Indian villages, and the Indians were friendly. Clark said Sacagawea had a lot to do with that. Her presence "reconsiles all the Indians as to our friendly intentions a woman with a party of men is a token of peace." The baby was an added benefit.

Sacagawea provided the same reassurance when the boats hit the Columbia, after the Snake joined it at present-day Pasco, Washington. Clark had climbed a cliff to get a look at the surrounding country and while waiting for Lewis and the others to arrive, shot a crane. His shot apparently alarmed some Indians across the river, who ran to their lodges. Clark, with three of the men, crossed the river in their canoe to where there were five lodges. There wasn't an Indian in sight, and when he pulled open the mat covering the entrance to one he found thirty-two terrified men, women and children huddled inside, "some crying and ringing there hands." The same was true in the other lodges. He offered them some trinkets and smoked with them, but none would go outside with him. Then Lewis arrived in his canoe with Sacagawea and Baptiste and "as soon as they Saw the Squar wife of the interperter they pointed to her and informed those who continued yet in the Same position I first found them, they imediately all came out and appeared to assume new life the sight of This Indian woman, wife to one of our interprs. confirmed those people of our friendly intentions, as no woman ever accompanies a war party of Indians in this quarter."

The party continued downstream. The rapids were fearsome. At Celilo Falls the river dropped thirty-eight feet in a short distance. The party portaged around part, with hired Indians and their horses to help, and at other spots they lowered the canoes through the rapids by ropes. At The Dalles, they decided, awful as the rapids were, that the rocky ledges flanking them were too rugged to carry the canoes across. The non-swimmers were sent ashore with the most valuable equipment. Indians, expert canoists themselves, gathered by the hundreds to watch the white men try something they wouldn't do; the prospect of picking up the pieces after the white men drowned was enticing. But the canoists made it. And again over the next stretch of rapids.

Finally, they arrived at the last rapids, as bad or worse than the ones they'd already passed; one set dropped twenty feet, at what today is Cascade Locks, Oregon. But they got down them, through portaging in places, lowering by rope in others. (All of these rapids on the Columbia have disappeared, flooded by waters backed up by dams).

Now it was an unobstructed run to the Pacific—and into the rain. "we are all wet and disagreeable, as we have been continually for several days past," Clark wrote. Adding to their misery was that "The swells were so high and the canoes roled in such a manner as to cause several to be verry sick. Reuben fields, Wiser McNeal & the Squar wer of the number." No mention whether Baptiste was seasick too, but then babies throw up all the time anyway.

That same day, November 7, Clark recorded in his notebook one of the greatest lines in American history: *"Ocian in view! O! the joy."*

There's some question whether the ocean actually was in view when Clark made his notation, but rather that the company was looking at the four-mile-wide estuary, which was roiled with waves.

But they were close enough; his exultation was warranted.

The Corps of Discovery had made it, 4,142 miles from the mouth of the Missouri, Clark figured.

Maybe because she was cold and wet—the rain hadn't stopped—a few days later Sacagawea got angry at Clark. Although he didn't record the reason, he did register it: "(squar displeased with me…)."

She showed she was a bona fide member of the company when some Indians came into their camp, one of whom was wearing a robe made of two sea otter skins "more butifull than any fur I had ever Seen," Clark said. Lewis and Clark both tried to buy it, offering him "many things," including a blanket and a coat, for the robe. He refused until Sacagawea, voluntarily or otherwise, gave up a belt of blue beads that she wore around her waist. The next day the captains gave her a coat of blue cloth, in exchange.

No hard feelings, apparently. A few days later Sacagawea gave Clark "a piece of bread made of flour which She had reserved for her child and carefully Kept until this time...which I eate with great satisfaction it being the only mouthful I had tasted for Several months past."

The company camped on the north shore of the Columbia in a miserable spot; the beach was narrow, and at high tide the waves kept rolling into camp. Clark, for one, was heartily sick of the ocean by now; it roared like repeated rolling thunder and had been for the twenty-four days since the expedition arrived. Since "we arrived in sight of the Great Western Ocian, I cant say Pasific as since I have seen it, it has been the reverse." There was little game, they wanted something more than dried fish for the winter, the company's clothes were rotting and they needed skins to replace them. At the same time they needed to stay near the mouth of the Columbia in case a trading ship came in; they badly needed a fresh supply of trinkets for trading with the Indians. The Indians were familiar with these vessels, having beads, buckles and other trinkets, blankets and clothes they'd gotten from traders.They'd also picked up some English from the sailors. Lewis reported they could repeat many words, such as "musquidt, powder, shot, nife, file, damned rascal, sun of a bitch &c." (One of the enduring mysteries of the Lewis and Clark Expedition is why Jefferson didn't send a ship to rendezvous with the company. In fact the vessel Lydia, out of Boston, did put into the Columbia while the company was in the area. The Lydia has just come down from Nootka Sound on Vancouver Island, where it had rescued John Jewitt, an Englishman who had been a captive of the Nootka Indians for three years. He was one of the two survivors of the

English trading ship Boston; the Indians had massacred the other twenty-eight of the crew; just fifteen years earlier the great English explorer, Captain James Cook, and his crew of the vessel Resolution had spent nearly a month there without serious problems. Clatsop Indians told the Lydia's captain that some white men had been there, and showed him medals the visitors had given them. But they also told him—according to Jewitt's translation, at least—that the white men, obviously Lewis and Clark, had left, when, in fact, they were just across the bay. And, for whatever reason, they didn't tell Lewis or Clark that the ship was there. So the opportunity for a ride home was lost. However, historian James Ronda says he's found evidence that the Lydia arrived two weeks *before* the expedition left for home). In early December the company moved across the Columbia into a small bay and then up a small river now called the Lewis and Clark. There they found elk and they built a log stockade fifty feet square with seven small cabins and prepared to spend the winter.

Lewis had found the spot for the new camp, but before the company moved, the captains called for a vote on where to locate for the winter. All members voted, including the slave York and Sacagawea, with the majority favoring crossing the bay to examine Lewis's location. The Indian woman wanted a place with plenty of "Potas,"—roots— probably Sauvie's island at the mouth of the Willamette far upriver, where on the way down she'd dug wappato. In his book Dr. Chuinard comments "The first suffragette vote in Oregon! The Oregon Suffragettes who used Sacagawea as a rallying symbol failed to mention their heroine had voted in the Oregon country one hundred years before—in the U.S. Army!" It also was the first time a slave voted.

In reporting that vote, Clark referred to Sacagawea as "Janey," the first time it was recorded as such in the journals. No explanation for the nickname; maybe Clark got tired of trying to spell her Indian name.

A fairly lively debate has sprung up in recent years about that vote. Some Lewis and Clark buffs, particularly ex-military men, have discounted it as only a gesture by the captains to encourage esprit de corps. They argue that, the captains already having decided upon the new location, if the troops had voted against it, the Expedition still would have crossed the river. But in any case, the majority *did* approve the move.

Christmas was a pretty drab affair, although the men woke the captains by shooting off their guns, shouting and singing. Clark commented that "we would have Spent this day the nativity of Christ in feasting, had we any thing either to raise our Sperits or even gratify our appetites, our Diner concisted of pore Elk, so much Spoiled that we eate it thro' mear necessity, Some pounded fish and a fiew roots." Private Whitehouse was more cheerful. "We had no ardent sperits of any kind among us; but are mostly in good health, a blessing, which we esteem more, than all the luxuries this life can afford, and the party are all thankful to the Supreme Being, for his goodness towards us, hoping he will preserve us in the same & enable us to return to the United States again in safety."

And there were presents. Clark got a shirt, drawers, and socks from Lewis. He violated that rule that officers don't take gifts from subordinates, by accepting a pair of "mockersons" from Whitehouse and a small Indian basket from Private Silas Goodrich.

But most interestingly of all, Sacagawea gave Clark "two dozen white weazils tails," striking because Christmas certainly wasn't an Indian celebration (although she'd watched the whites celebrate the previous Christmas at Fort Mandan) and its suggestion of growing fondness by the Indian woman for the white captain.

The New Year's celebration was limited. The men awoke the captains with a volley of gunfire. No other celebration, no feast. The day, Lewis said, "consisted principally in the anticipation of the 1st day of January 1807," when the company would be back home with friends and family.

The captains learned from the Indians that a whale had washed ashore south of the camp and decided to send a party of twelve to see it and get some blubber. Sacagawea wasn't included. But she showed spunk. On January 6, 1806 Lewis wrote that "Charbono and his Indian woman were also of the party; the Indian woman was very impotunate to be permitted to go, and was therefore indulged; she observed that she had traveled a long way with us to see the great waters, and that now that the monstrous fish was also to be seen, she thought it very hard she could not be permitted to see either (she had never yet been to the Ocean)."

So she and Baptiste, now eleven months old, made the trip, which was a hard one; thirty-five miles south over precipitous Tillamook Head to what is today's Cannon Beach. The whale wasn't much more than a skeleton by the time the party got there but it brought back three hundred pounds of blubber. That trip was the highlight of the winter.

The captains spent much of the winter working on their reports, Lewis on the scientific aspects, Clark on his maps of the route from Fort Mandan to Fort Clatsop. Lewis, after reviewing the maps, concluded, "We now discover that we have found the most practicable and navigable passage across the Continent of North America." What that meant was a big disappointment, the dashing of the principle hope of the expedition, that of finding an all-water route across the continent. The short portage from the Missouri to the Columbia was an illusion.

No Passage to China.

At 1 p.m. on March 23, after stealing a canoe from the Clatsops, the expedition started home in five canoes. They'd had a miserable winter. While there was enough to eat, they'd gotten tired of elk. It had rained nearly every day; in fact the return was postponed several days because it was raining and blowing so hard. And there

28

had been many cases of venereal disease. Lewis treated the men with mercury although the Journals don't explain how. Dr. Chuinard says the usual method was to apply salves that included mercury to the lesions.

When the company got to Celilo Falls, the captains decided it would be impossible to get the canoes past them—although it had gotten them down—and bought ten horses. Only one person rode, Private William Bratton this time; his back hurt so bad he couldn't walk. On April 27 they reached the Wallawalla Indians at their camp about twelve miles below the junction of the Columbia and the Snake, and Sacagawea's languages again came into use. They had a captive Shoshone woman. She could speak to Sacagawea, who passed it on to Charbonneau who passed it on to George Drouillard, who could speak English; he passed it to the captains. Then the conversation went back in reverse order.

The chief of the tribe, Yellept, gave Clark "a very eligant white horse." In return Clark presented the chief with his sword and a hundred balls and powder. The party bought more horses from the Wallawallas, bringing their total to twenty-three. The price was high and the expedition had about run out of goods for trade. Lewis gave up his custom-made personal dueling pistol.

In early May the corps reached the Nez Perce Indians, on the Clearwater, to get bad news. The heavy snow in the mountains would delay crossing the Rockies. As it turned out, the company was stuck until June 10.

The time was spent in trading for food for the grueling trip across the mountains, in foot and horse races with the Indians—the Indians usually won—and in Clark treating the Indians for a variety of ailments.

One of the patients was Sacagawea's child Baptiste, now fifteen months old. On May 22, Lewis recorded that "Charbono's Child is very ill this evening; he is cutting teeth, and for several days past has had a violent lax, which having suddonly stopped he was attached with a high fever and his neck and throat are

29

much swolen this evening, we gave him a doze of creem of tartar and flour of sulpher and applyed a poltice of boiled onions to his neck as warm as he could well bear it."

The next day Lewis reported that the boy was "considerably better" after "the Creem of tartar and sulpher operated several times on the child in the course of last night" although the swelling had gone down only slightly. Poltices of onions were continued, day and night. But the next day he reported that the boy was "very wrestless last night" and that his jaw and the back of his neck were more swollen than the day before although his fever had gone down. More cream of tartar and poltices of onions.

The following day Baptiste was even worse. The tartar didn't work, so they gave him a "clyster," a medicinal enema, apparently. And the next day Lewis reported that the boy was better. "The Clyster given the Child last evening operated very well." He was clear of fever and the swelling had diminished. Lewis thought the inflamation would "pass off" without coming to a head, although the onion poltices continued.

For the next three days the journals report steady improvement in Baptiste, although Clark thought the swelling would "termonate in an ugly imposthume [abcess] a little below the ear."

By June 8, both Lewis and Clark reported that the boy was nearly well although the lump on his neck remained swollen and hard.

That this appears to be the only time that Baptiste was ill on the whole trip is remarkable considering what the child had been through—snow, freezing weather, months of soaking rain, an escape from drowning. There is only one other mention in the journals of his well-being. In early August, when the expedition was on the Missouri, Clark noted that "The child of Shabono has been so much bitten by the Musquetors that his face is much puffed up & Swelled."

Dr. Chuinard, writing more than one hundred and seventy years after Baptiste's sickness, thought the boy may have had mastoiditis. Elliott Coues, in his history of the expedition, thought it might have been mumps. No one today knows. But it was serious. Dr. Chuinard said, based upon the journal entries, there was no doubt he was near death. "His recovery must be attributed to her [Sacagawea] mother's care and his endurance and natural resistance, as well as to the prescriptions of the captain-physicians," both of whom ministered to the boy.

Food was a constant problem. The journals record that Sacagawea was busy for days gathering roots, some of which apparently cured headaches and colic that the soldiers were complaining about. The expedition's members had become fond of eating dog, which the Nez Perce held in contempt, and at one meal a young brave threw a puppy at Lewis. Lewis threw it back and shook his tomahawk at the brave, who "withdrew apparently much mortified." (Other Indian tribes weren't so persnickety. On the trail they turned their dogs into small pack animals, carrying moccasins and other light supplies. When they were used up, the Indians ate the dogs.) The Indians treated by Clark paid the bill with horses, which the company killed and ate.

Finally, although the Indians warned them the snow was still too deep, the captains decided to start across the mountains, fearing that if they didn't get going they'd never made it to the United States that year. They loaded up with as many provisions as they could buy. The captains even cut the buttons off their coats to trade for roots and root bread. On June 15 the party set out.

But the Indians were right.The snow was twelve to fifteen feet deep and the trail over the Lolo Pass was uncertain. Drouillard, whom the captains used as their main guide, "was entirely doubtfull." Worried that without Indian guides, they'd become hopelessly lost, they turned back, "melancholy and discouraged." It was a hard retreat. Private John Colter's horse fell with him aboard while crossing

Hungry Creek and they rolled over each other "a considerable distance" on the rocks. Colter hung onto his gun but lost his blanket. Private John Potts badly cut his leg with a knife; Lewis had a hard time stopping the bleeding.

It wasn't until June 24 that the company set off again, this time with three Nez Perce guides. The snow was melting; in one spot where it had been eleven feet deep it was down to seven. By June 30 the party reached the camp where it had stopped the previous September, which it called Traveller's Rest (near present Missoula, Montana). The company had covered one hundred fifty-six miles in six days. The previous year, going the other direction, it had taken eleven days.

The trip had been hazardous, with steep climbs and descents over the mountains. At one point Lewis's horse slipped off the track, Lewis fell off and slid forty feet before he grabbed a branch. "The horse was near falling on me," he wrote. But it didn't, and both man and horse escaped injury. They ran out of food; one day lunch was "bear's oil with some boiled roots."

It was here the captains decided to split the company in a complicated plan that would permit Lewis to do some further exploring. He, with nine men and seventeen horses, would follow the Nez Perce Indian trail to the Great Falls of the Missouri. There he would leave three men to dig up the cache buried the previous year and take the other six to go up the Marias River. Clark, with ten men, including Toussaint Charbonneau, and with Sacagawea (and Baptiste, of course) and the servant slave York, would cross the Continental Divide to the Yellowstone River, build canoes and then go down the river to its meeting with the Missouri, where the expedition would rejoin.

That's what happened. Except Lewis, with his very small party, ran into the Blackfeet Indians. When that meeting was over, Reubin Fields had stabbed to death one Indian who was stealing Fields's rifle and Lewis shot another, who, though probably fatally wounded, fired at Lewis. "Being bearheaded I felt the wind of his bullet very distinctly," he wrote.

The killing of the Blackfeet had serious long-term effects for Americans. The tribe became the most fearsome opponents of the trappers and traders who invaded the mountains after the expedition, attacking and killing them without provacation other than their just being there. With long memories, the Blackfeet called the invaders "Big Knives." This by a tribe that had traded peacefully with the Canadians for years before it ran into Lewis.

Lewis and party got out of there as fast as they could. At the mouth of the Marias, they retrieved the perogue and the five small canoes that had been cached there in 1805, and headed down the Missouri.

But not without another incident, this one painful. After reaching the Missouri, Lewis and Private Peter Cruzatte went elk hunting. By accident Cruzatte shot Lewis. The bullet hit him on the left lower side, passing through his buttocks and coming out the right side. The wound plagued Lewis for a month.

Meanwhile, Sacagawea did, in fact, provide service as a guide. The Clark party was travelling up a road used by the Flathead Indians, a better and shorter route than the expedition had used the previous autumn.

Although the track disappeared, Sacagawea recognized the spot at once; she told Clark she'd been there often as a child as the place to gather roots and to catch beaver. When they reached the higher part of the plain, she said, they would see a gap in the mountains through which they should pass. Clark followed her directions and on July 8, the party reached the Two Forks of the Jefferson River, where they'd cached supplies the previous year, including tobacco. For that, the men who chewed tobacco were so anxious, Clark wrote, "they scarcely took the saddles from their horses before they ran to the cave and were delighted at being able to resume this fascinating indulgence."

Two days later they loaded the canoes they had left with the baggage and one group started down the river. Clark, with the second group, including Sacagawea, went on horseback. They had passed the Three Forks of the Missouri, which was near where she'd been captured as a child and had come to a spot where two tracks led to passes in the mountains. "The Indian woman who has been of great service to me as a pilot through this country recommends a gap in the mountains more south, which I shall cross," Clark wrote. It was the opening now called Bozeman Pass.

The party moved on to the Yellowstone River. Clark had two twenty-eight-foot canoes built, lashed them side by side, and the party started the last leg of their incredible journey. When they saw an unusual rock, some two hundred feet high, on the south side of the river, they stopped and Clark carved his name and the date: July 25, 1806. The carvings can still be seen. Clark also named the rock Pompy's Tower, (now called Pompey's Pillar), after the nickname of young Baptiste Charbonneau. It was along here that the mosquitoes bit him so badly his face was swollen. They were so thick that when Clark tried to shoot a bighorn sheep, he couldn't keep them "from the barrel of his rifle long enough to take aim."

Some odd stories about Pompey's Pillar developed. One was that it was named after Clark's slave; somebody thought his name was Pompey, not York. Another was that it was named after a steamboat hand who died and was buried on the top of the pillar. But it was many years after the expedition before a steamboat, with hands, went up the Yellowstone. Olin D. Wheeler, author of "The Trail of Lewis and Clark," published in 1904, had the definitive answer. "Undoubtedly it was named for the historic pile at Alexandria, Egypt, but which it does not resemble in the least." He was wrong, too. There can be no doubt that the rock was named for Baptiste Charbonneau. Clark called the Indian child by that nickname and, years later, called one of his own sons Pomp. The only question, not very important, is when and why Pompy's Tower, which is what Clark twice called it in his journal, became Pompey's Pillar. It probably happened because Nicholas Biddle, who wrote the two-volume narrative of the expedition published in 1814, recorded, inaccurately, that Clark had named it Pompey's Pillar, adding the "e" and making it a pillar rather than a tower. That was the name of the monument to a Roman general in Egypt, and Biddle, unaware of Baptiste's nickname, must have thought that was what Clark had in mind.

Clark's party moved onto the Missouri and headed downstream.

On August 12, Lewis's party caught up with Clark, who found his colleague lying face down in the peroque, nursing his wound. In two more days, moving rapidly down the swift-flowing river, the company arrived at the Mandan Indian villages.

For Sacagawea, Baptiste, now nineteen months old, and Toussaint Charbonneau it was the end of a three thousand nine hundred-mile adventure.

But not a very profitable one. Charbonneau was paid off, "for his services as an enterpreter the price of a horse and a Lodge purchased of him for public Service in all" the grand total of $500.33 and one-third cents.

Sacagawea, whom by any reasonable accounting was of far more value to the expedition than her husband, got nothing.

Clark did offer to take the three to St. Louis. Charbonneau declined, saying that "hed had no acquaintance or prospects of makeing a liveing below, and must continue to live in the way he had done." Clark then offered to take just Baptiste, "a butifull promising child" with him to educate. That, too, was declined, although both Sacagawea and Toussaint would have been willing if the boy had been weaned. In a year, they told Clark, he would be old enough to leave his mother. At that time Charbonneau would be willing to bring him to Clark "if I would be so friendly as to raise the child for him in such a manner as I thought proper, to which I agreed &c."

Charbonneau would have made the trip to St. Louis and beyond as translator if the captains had been able to persuade the Minnetare chiefs to go to Washington to meet their Great White Father, President Jefferson. But the Indians refused. A Mandan chief, Big White, did agree and so the captains took along the chief, his wife and two children and Rene Jessaume, hired as translator, and his wife and two children.

The party, after many parleys and smokes with the Indians, pushed off on the final chapter of their odyssey on August 18. There were brief stops along the way; one was to buy a gallon of whiskey from a passing trader, giving each man a dram "which is the first spiritous licquor which had been tasted by any of them since the 4 of July 1805." The corps arrived at St. Louis about noon on September 23, 1806, twenty-eight months and more than seven thousaand miles after it started up the Missouri.

The rest of the men were paid off, at rates ranging from $25 a month, for the interpreter George Drouillard, to $5 for the enlisted men. (In 1807, Congress passed a bill to, in effect, double their pay and to give each man warrants for three hundred and twenty acres of land. Charbonneau received another $409.16 and 2/3 cents, and a warrant for the land. There's no record that he ever exercised it but he may have. In 1843, in settling Toussaint's estate, Baptiste sold land he'd inherited from his father for $320; that suggests it was the land acquired by the warrant, sold at $1 an acre. Clark's black slave York received nothing. He asked Clark for his freedom. His request was refused. (Clark finally freed him ten years later).

There were only two men missing from the original upriver party. On reaching the Mandan Indian villages on the return trip Private John Colter decided to quit to go trapping. Also missing was Sergeant Charles Floyd, who had died of appendicitis on the first leg of the journey, the only man to die on the greatest American expedition in history.

In the years that followed, ten states that the explorers traveled were added to the union: Missouri, Kansas, Nebraska, Iowa, North and South Dakota, Montana, Idaho, Washington and Oregon.

On September 26, 1806, Captain Clark recorded one of the great understatements in American historiography: "a fine morning we commenced wrighting &c."

3

THE CHARBONNEAU FAMILY BREAKS UP

Two days after the Lewis and Clark Expedition left the Mandan Indian villages headed down the Missouri for St. Louis, it met traders headed upstream. William Clark handed the traders an extraordinary letter he'd written while being paddled down the river, to be delivered back to the villages:

> On Board the Perogue Near the Ricara Village
>
> August 20th, 1806
>
> *Charbono*
>
> Sir
>
> Your present situation with the Indians gives me some concern—I wish now I had advised you to come on with me to the Illinois where it would most probably be in my power to put you on some way to do something for yourself...you have been a long time with me and have conducted yourself in such a manner

as to gain my friendship; your woman, who accompanied you that long dangerous and fatiguing route to the Pacific ocean and back, deserved a greater reward for her attention and services on that route than we had in our power to give her at the Mandans. As to your little son (my boy *Pomp*) you well know my fondness for him and my anxiety to take and raise him as my own child. I once more tell you if you will bring Baptiste to me, I will educate him and treat him as my own child—I do not forget the promise which I made to you and shall now repeat them that you may be certain—Charbono, if you wish to live with the white people and will come to me, I will give you a piece of land and furnish you with horses cows and hogs—If you wish to visit your friends in *Montrall* I will let you have a horse, and your family shall be taken care of until your return—if you wish to return as an interpreter for the Menetarras when the troops come to form the establishment, you will be with me ready and I will procure you the place—or if you wish to return to trade with the Indians and will leave your little *son Pomp* with me, I will assist you with merchandise for that purpose, and become myself concerned with you in trade on a small scale, that is to say not exceeding a perogue load at one time. If you are disposed to accept either of my offers to you, and will bring down your son, your famn Janey had best come along with you to take care of the boy until I get him—let me advise you to keep your bill of exchange and what furs and pelteries you have in possession, and get as much as you can collect in the course of this winter. And take them down to St. Louis as early as possible. Enquire of the governor of that place for a letter I shall leave with the governor. I shall inform you what you had best do with your furs pelteries and robes, etc. when you get to St. Louis write a letter to me by the post and let me know your situation—If you do not intend to go down either this fall or in the spring, write a letter to me by the first opportunity and inform me what you intend to do that I may know if I may expect you or not. If you ever intend to come down this fall or next spring will be the best time—this fall would be best if you could get down before the winter. I shall be found either in St. Louis or in Clarksville at the falls of the Ohio.

Wishing you and your family great success, and with anxious expectations of seeing my little dancing boy, Baptiste, I shall remain your friend.

WILLIAM CLARK

As if the letter with its strangely pleading tone wasn't odd enough, Clark then added an even odder postscript:

Keep this letter and let not more than one or two persons see it, and when you write to me seal your letter. I think you best not determine which of my offers to accept until you see me. Come prepared to accept of either which you may chuse after you get down.

Mr. Teousant Charbono
Minetarras Village

Clark had offered almost everything in his power to entice Charbonneau—and his wife and most particularly his child—to St. Louis: he'd give him a farm and livestock; or go into business with him, or fix him a job as a translator with the

Minnetares when army troops built a fort at the villages. But he wanted his offers kept secret: "let not more than one or two persons see" his letter.

One can only speculate why. The suggestion of influence peddling—"I will procure you the place"—wouldn't have seemed that damning in 1806 (or today, for that matter); Charbonneau obviously was qualified as a translator. Maybe Clark was embarrassed about his desire to have the company of the child. Possibly he didn't want known his favoring of one member of the expedition over all the others.

In any case, even if Charbonneau and Sacagawea saw the letter—since it was in English, somebody would have had to read it to them—they were unmoved.

But two years later they took Clark up on his offer and moved to St. Louis, where Clark had been appointed Superintendent of Indian Affairs by President Jefferson. There, on December 28, 1809, in an old log church, Baptiste was baptized by a Trappist monk, Father Urbain Guillet. The child was almost five years old.

At least, it is highly likely it was Baptiste who was baptized that winter day; the baptismal record doesn't name him. What it does say is that "The year eighteen hundred nine the twenty-eighth of December, I, brother Urbain Guillet Reu of the Trappist monastery of Our Lady of Good Help near Cahokia, in the Illinois Territory, baptized a child born the eleventh of February in the year eighteen hundred four of Toussaint Charboneau, living in this parish and of"—at this point there is a blank in the certificate where the mother's name should be, and then it adds, as identification of the mother—"savage of the Snake Nation." Except that the certificate is in French and thus puts it more poetically: "Sauvagesse de la nation des Serpents."

So the record, which was only recently discovered by Bob Moore, the historian at the Jefferson National Expansion Memorial in St. Louis, in the Register of Baptisms of the Old Cathedral Parish of St. Louis, has the year of birth wrong for Baptiste—he was born in 1805, not 1804, as the Journals amply record and the mother's name is missing. (There appears to be no provision in the baptismal record for the child's name). But since the record correctly cites the birth day, and identifies the mother as a Snake, and names the father, this must be the record of Baptiste's baptism.

Moore suggests that Father Guillet, as a foreigner—he was Swiss—and a member of an ascetic order, had no knowledge of the parents and their links with the Lewis and Clark Expedition, or of the expedition itself for that matter. He simply was doing his duty.

As interesting as the record itself is the name of the godfather, Auguste Chouteau.

Auguste Chouteau was a big man in St. Louis. At age fourteen his stepfather put him in charge of the party that cleared the land for the town, preparatory to settlement. He became a dominant figure in the fur trade. For a man of that stature to be godfather to a half-Indian boy must have been unusual. It suggests that Clark, the most important man in the territory (who missed the ceremony because he was in Washington) may have asked Chouteau to perform the function. Or maybe he did it because Charbonneau was French. Four years later he would hire Toussaint for a trading trip to Santa Fe.

Toussaint Charbonneau tried to settle down. He bought a tract of land just outside St. Louis from Clark and tried to farm. It didn't take. He sold the land the next year back to Clark, for $100, and headed back to Indian country, taking Sacagawea with him but leaving Baptiste, now six years old, to be educated by Clark.

In St. Louis the interpreter and his Indian wife boarded a barge owned by Manuel Lisa, the premier trader of the day, headed for the fort named after him, which had been built on the Missouri downstream from the Mandan Indian villages. Aboard that barge was Henry M. Brackenridge, out to see the West. In his journal he wrote that he met "a Frenchman named Charbonet and his Indian wife, who had accompanied Lewis and Clark to the Pacific. The woman, a good creature, of a mild and gentle disposition, greatly attached to the whites, whose manners and dress she tries to imitate, but she had become sickly and longed to revisit her native country; her husband also, who had spent many years amongst the Indians, was become weary of a civilized life."

A year later John C. Luttig, who was in charge of Fort Manuel, made a laconic entry in his journal. On December 20, 1812 he noted first that the weather was clear and moderate, that he had purchased "a fine Dog," and then that "this Evening the Wife of Charbonneau a Snake Squaw, died of a putrid fever she was a good and the best Women in the fort, aged abt 25 years she left a fine infant girl."

Thus Sacagawea, the young Indian woman who had trekked across the country and back with very little complaint, survived a serious illness and many hardships, died an untimely death and passed into American lore.

Luttig would have saved a lot of contention in later years if he had named the "Wife of Charbonneau" who died. But considering all the evidence known then and later there can be little doubt it was Sacagawea.

Early the following year, Fort Manuel had to be abandoned after Indian attacks that killed fifteen members of Lisa's company. Luttig, as well as Lisa and others, retreated to St. Louis, and Luttig brought along Lizette, apparently the infant daughter of Sacagawea and Toussaint Charbonneau; the latter, who wasn't at Fort Manuel when the attacks happened, was assumed to be dead. Because in August of 1813, an order was entered in Orphan's Court, St. Louis:

"The court appoints John C. Luttig guardian to the infant children of Tousant Charbonneau deceased, to wit: Tousant Charbonneau, a boy of about the age of ten years; and Lizette Charbonneau, a girl about one year old. The said infant children not being possessed of any property within the knowledge of the court, the said guardian is not required to give bond."

But Luttig's name was crossed out on the document and the name of William Clark, now Governor of the Louisiana Territory as well as Superintendent of Indian Affairs, was substituted.

(Although the court order referred to the child as "Tousant Charbonneau," it wasn't unusual for children to be known by their father's name. The document also was incorrect on two other points: the boy was eight years old, not ten, and the senior Charbonneau most definitely wasn't deceased).

The half-Indian child was now a ward of the man who on the great expedition had so taken a fancy to "my litle dancing boy, Baptiste."

Nothing more is known of Lizette.

A great deal more is known about Baptiste's father, Toussaint Charbonneau. Despite Meriwether Lewis damning him with faint praise, Toussaint went on after his incompetent performance on the expedition to lead a long life as an interpreter and sometime trader and trapper.

Lewis, in a letter recommending bonuses to the men of the expedition, described Toussaint Charbonneau as "A man of no peculiar merit; was useful as an interpreter only," although he did add that in that capacity he "discharged his duties with good faith." Charbonneau certainly showed singular ineptness when he was on the trail. His panic that nearly sank the perogue already has been documented. That was the second time his incompetance at the helm had nearly upset the boat. After that second time, he was relieved of helmsman duties. But the Journals are replete with reports of his incompetence. On June 2, out hunting with George Drouillard [which the Journals consistently spell Drewyer], a grizzly took after Charbonneau, who in panic fired his gun in the air rather than at the bear, and then ran and hid in the bushes while Drouillard killed it with a shot in the head. At the end of June occurred the flash flood which could have killed Clark, Sacagawea, Baptiste and Charbonneau; they were saved only by Clark's wits, strength and courage. Clark reported that while he was trying to pull the Indian woman and her baby up the ravine, "the Interpreter himself makeing attempts to pull his wife by the hand much scared and nearly without motion."

The next month Charbonneau injured his ankle and was "unable to proceede any further." Six days later, the translator wanted to hike along with Clark, saying his ankle was much better, although Clark doubted that. He went and a few days later Clark said that Charbonneau was complaining about his leg and "is the cause of considerable detention to us." A day later Charbonneau was still complaining and Clark told him to proceed at his leisure.

Clark got disgusted: "Some words with Sharbono our interpreter about his duties."

On the way home the next year, Charbonneau's pack horse ran away and dumped and lost most of its load and twice in the next four days the expedition was delayed because he failed to hobble his horses and they ran away. One of them was never recovered.

But he survived the trip.

For more than forty years he lived, off and on, in the Minnetaree and Mandan Indian villages on the Missouri, working for the major figures in the booming fur trade and as an interpreter for government Indian agents. He was employed by the American Fur Company, the Missouri Fur Company, of which William Clark was president, and the Columbia Fur Company. And he spent a year with Auguste P. Chouteau & Company, an important fur trading firm, on a trapping and trading trip along the Platte and Arkansas.

That trip was a disaster. The Chouteau brigade, which was lead by Chouteau himself, fell victim to the shifting views of the Spanish government about trade with the Americans. Chouteau had expected to take his furs to trade in Santa Fe. Instead, Spanish troops surrounded the brigade, forced the Americans to march to Santa Fe, confiscated their furs and threw them into jail. After forty-eight days they were kicked out of the country and all their possessions taken, except for one horse each. After the return to the United States, Chouteau applied to the U.S. Government for reparations of $30,000; the records are silent on whether he got it. But in connection with that petiton, Charbonneau filed an affidavit—signed with his mark since he was illiterate—that he'd signed on with Chouteau & Company in July, 1816 for the trading expedition on the Platte and Arkansas, that he was going to be paid $200, that he made the expedition and was with the company until July, 1817. It isn't clear from the affidavit whether he was imprisoned in Santa Fe but the circumstances certainly suggest that he was.

For twenty years, from 1819 to 1839, Charbonneau was an employe of U.S. Indian agents and subagents. As a result, he was well known in the mountain trade, both favorably and unfavorably. In 1823 Prince Paul Friedrich Wilhelm, Duke of Wurttemberg, on the first of his five tours of America, hired Charbonneau briefly as his interpreter. Toussaint apparently served him satisfactorily, because he hired him again on his second tour, in 1830. Account books of the time show that the Prince purchased several items, including tobacco and powder, as gifts for Toussaint. In 1832 Prince Maximillian of Wied, another of the foreign tourists who came tramping through the west after the Lewis and Clark Expedition, found Charbonneau very helpful as an interpreter and in explaining Indian customs to him. The Prince also noted that after thirty-seven years of living with the Minnetarees, Touissant admitted he still couldn't speak their language very well. He served as interpreter for the artists Karl Bodmer and George Catlin, among other notables, on their western travels.

He also gained renown as a cook; there are repeated references in trapper and trader journals to the fine meals he prepared. Early on the expedition Lewis described at length a dish that Charbonneau prepared, which he called a *boudin (poudingue) blanc,* made from a stuffed buffalo gut, "baptised in the missouri with two dips and a flirt," then "fryed with bears oil untill it becomes brown, when it is ready to esswage the pangs of a keen appetite..." Francis Chardon at Fort Clark, which was at the Mandan Indian villages and was the principal trading post for the Mandans and Hidatsas, recorded in 1836 that "Charboneau gave us a feast of Mince pie and Coffee—which was excellent."

But John Luttig, who was managing Fort Manuel in 1812, complained bitterly about him. Charbonneau and Rene Jessaume, the French-Canadian who had translated for Lewis and Clark with the Mandans, "Keep us in Constant uproar with their Histories and wish to make fear among the Engagees, these two Rascals ought to be hung for their perfidy, they do more harm than good to the American Government, stir up the Indians and pretend to be friends to the white People at the same time but we find them to be our Ennemies," he wrote. Luttig also accused Charbonneau of cowardice. He recorded that Indians had driven off seven of the fort's horses and that "Charbonneau who was on horse back came in full speed and cried out; *To Arms* Lecomte is Killed, he run off and left the poor fellow..." Francoise Lecompte was one of the traders, he wasn't killed—the Indians let him go—and the Indians didn't attack the camp.

Luttig said that even the Indians didn't like him. Some Arikaras arrived "which were enraged against Charbonneau & Jessaume, having heard of their arrival from the Bigbellies they said that C. & J. were Lyars and not to be considered as good french men, and if Mr. Manuel Lisa would send them to the Grosventer with a pipe they would not consent such Credit have these Men amongst the Indians—they find their Character gone and try every Scheme, to Keep themselves alive, like a Men a drowning."

In 1834, trader William Laidlaw wrote to James Kipp after learning Kipp had hired Charbonneau as an interpreter at Fort Clark, "...I am much surprised at your taking Old Charboneau into favor after showing so much ingratitude, upon all occasions (the old Knave, what does he say for himself."

To the end, Charbonneau fancied young Indian women. Chardon reported that "Charboneau and his lady started for the Gros Ventres on a visit (or to tell you the truth) in quest for one of his runaway wives—for I must inform you he had two lively ones. Poor old man."

In 1837 Chardon recorded that one of Charbonneau's wives, unnamed, died of smallpox at the Mandan villages; she was one of the first victims of the plague that was sweeping up the river. It appears to have been introduced to the Indians this time by an infected passenger aboard the steamer St. Peters. (There had been an outbreak in the early 1800s). Before it was over there were fewer than two hundred—Historian Bernard DeVoto says barely more than a hundred—Mandans left alive, out of a tribe of sixteen hundred. Although his two-year-old son died, Chardon, who didn't like Indians even though he made his living trading with them, wasn't terribly upset by the death toll: "What a band of RASCALS has been used up," he wrote. Thousands of Indians of other tribes also died.

Some of his colleagues liked Charbonneau. Chardon described the last sexual exploit recorded anywhere about the interpreter. At eighty or thereabouts, he took as a wife a fourteen-year-old Assiniboine who had been captured by the Arikaras—the Rees—and the men of the fort "gave to the old man a splendid Chariveree the drums, pans, kittles, etc., beating, guns fireing, etc. the old gentleman gave a feast to the men, and a glass of grog—and went to bed with his young wife, with the intention of doing his best..." The Rees who sold her "had never seen the like before, were under the apprehension that we were for killing of them, and sneaked off."

There is one last account of Charbonneau. On August 26, 1839, Joshua Pilcher, Superintendent of Indian Affairs in St. Louis, wrote to headquarters that "Toussaint Charbonneau, the late Mandan Interpreter, arrived here from the Mandan villages, a distance of 1600 miles, and came into the office, tottering under the infirmities of 80 winters, without a dollar to support him..." It turned out that the department had decided to fire him after fifteen years as interpreter for the Mandan Indian agency at the end of 1838, probably because the agency had been decimated by smallpox. But the notice didn't reach him until July and he had faithfully worked through the first six months of 1839. Pilcher, a bureaucrat with heart, recommended that Charbonneau be paid for those six months and he was.

And there the record of the long career of Toussaint Charbonneau, husband of Sacagawea, father of Baptiste, veteran of the famous Corps of Discovery, Indian trader and interpreter with a colorful if eccentric past, damned by many, praised by a few, ends. He apparently was dead by 1843 because in August of that year, according to a document in the Sublette Papers, there was a promissory note, signed by a Francis Pensoneau of St. Louis, that read "I promise to pay to J.B. Charbonno the Sum of Three hundred and twenty dollars, as soon as I dispose of land Claimed by him said Charbonno from the estate of his Deceased Father."

An endorsement dated August 17, 1843, is signed by J.B. Charbonneau, "To be paid W.A. Sublette."

So the old reprobate left, maybe inadvertently, a small legacy to his only known son, possibly to make up a bit for gambling away the boy's horses years before. And Baptiste turned the money over to his old boss, probably in repayment for supplies. The land in question was that awarded Touissant for his services with the Corps of Discovery.

4

BAPTISTE GOES TO SCHOOL—AND TO EUROPE

It isn't certain how long Baptiste remained under Clark's wing in St. Louis. It is certain that he was in his care as late as 1820. One writer places him in the Minnetaree village where Toussaint Charbonneau and Sacagawea lived before and after the expedition, when the boy was ten or eleven years old. It is possible that Baptiste did go back to his native village for visits before returning to St. Louis. The writer related how the father took Baptiste's favorite horse—he'd already lost by gambling three others belonging to the boy—and promptly lost that one, too.

If the story was true, that would have been about 1815. The writer was James Willard Schultz, author of *Bird Woman, Sacagawea's Own Story,* originally published in 1918, more than one hundred years after the events in question. Schultz claimed to have gotten the eyewitness account from a fur trader named Hugh Monroe in the 1880s—when Monroe himself was in his eighties. Monroe said he had a long conversation with Sacagawea, who also was there, in French. But Sacagawea almost certainly had been dead for several years in 1815 and didn't speak French, as the translation difficulties recounted in Lewis and Clark's Journals make clear.

The historian Grace Raymond Hebard called Schultz's book "purely historical fiction." But it has been frequently cited as a source for the period by other historians.

In her book, Hebard said she had letters from William Clark Kennerly, William Clark's nephew, who was raised in St. Louis, in which Kennerly said he frequently saw Sacagawea and Toussaint Charbonneau in the village, and that he knew Baptiste. Unfortunately, those letters can't be found and, and if they existed, surely were wrong.

James Haley White, who was about fifteen at the time, went to school with Baptiste. In his brief memoir, *St. Louis and Its Men Fifty Years Ago,* White told of attending class in the school run by the Rev.James E. Welch, a thirty-one-year-old Baptist missionary, at the corner of Third and Market Streets. He called Baptiste a "mestizo,"[mixed race] and for some reason thought that because his father was a French Canadian and his mother a Snake Indian he was "three quarters white and one quarter Indian."

White recounted how with Baptiste he often visited the museum that Willaim Clark had built onto his house, one that held "a large collection of Indian trinkets and relics collected during his expeditions," and where Clark greeted the many delegations from Indian tribes that came to him for settlement of their problems. Overhead hung a birch bark canoe. Baptiste told White he was born in the boat "and he has often when I visited the museum with him, pointed to the canoe calling it his cradle and telling its history," White wrote.

A lovely story, but the product of a youngster's imagination. Baptiste wasn't born in a canoe and Lewis and Clark didn't have birch bark canoes on their expedition.

Baptiste also took classes from the Rev. Francis Neil, a Catholic priest, who ran a boys school that later became St. Louis University.

Clark had moved to a farm outside town and so Baptiste boarded out at least part of the time with Clark paying the bills, although he may have passed them on to the government as Indian education. Existing records show the following for 1820:

Jan. 22, 1820. No. of vou.—118. Payments, to whom made—J.E. Welch. Nature of disbursements—for two quarters' tuition of J.B. Charboneau, a half Indian boy, and firewood and ink. Amount—$16.37 1/2.

March 31. L.T. Honore. For boarding, lodging, and washing of J.B. Charboneau, a half Indian, from 1st January to 31st March, 1820. Amount—$45.00.

April 11. J.E. Welch. For one quarter's tuition of J.B. Charboneau, a half Indian boy, including fuel and ink. Amount, $8.37 1/2.

May 17. F. Neil. For one quarter's tuition of Toussaint [Baptiste] Charboneau, a half Indian boy. Amount—$12.00.

June 30. L.T. Honore. For board and lodging and washing of J.B. Charboneau, a half Indian boy, from 1st April to 30th June. Amount—$45.00

Oct. 1. L.T. Honore. Nature of disbursements—For boarding, lodging and washing of J.B. Charboneau, from 1st July to 30th September, 1820, at $15 per month. Amount—$45.00.

And then there were bills for all those things a schoolboy needs:

April 1. J.&G.H. Kennerly. For one Roman History for Charboneau, a half Indian, $1.50; one pair of shoes for ditto, $2.25; two pair of socks for ditto, $1.50; two quires paper and quills for Charboneau, 1.50; (one Scott's lessons for ditto, $1.50; one dictionary for ditto, $1.50; one hat for ditto, $4.00; four yards of cloth for ditto, $10;)...one ciphering book, $1; one slate and pencils, 62 cents for Charboneau.

Though only a village of fifteen hundred people or so in 1815, St.Louis was booming as trade with the west opened up. The streets were filled with French, Spanish, blacks and Indians. One of the finest houses was owned by Auguste Chouteau, Baptiste's godfather, head of the family of successful fur trappers and traders. His house covered a whole square, surrounded by a ten-foot wall. St. Louis's population soared: forty-six hundred in 1820, eighty thousand in 1850.

Baptiste left St. Louis about 1821, his formal education completed, and moved up the Missouri to a settlement on the Kansas River, where he apparently was trapping for furs.

Enter twenty-six-year-old Prince Paul Friedrich Wilhelm, Duke of Wurttemberg, near Stuttgart. Prince Paul was a tourist of the first degree. From Hamburg he had sailed, slowly, to New Orleans, from there to Havana, Cuba, where he toured the country, and then back to New Orleans, then to Louisville on the Ohio, back down, and finally to St. Louis.

He wanted to travel west into Indian country. And so he applied to William Clark, who issued the permits that allowed such travels, with a very peculiar letter. After telling Clark that his sole purpose was the study of botany and natural history, he asked for a passport to visit "the region of the country bordering the Missoury and the Columbia rivers." He said that not knowing he would need a passport from Clark, he'd left most of his documents in New Orleans "which is certified by the American Counsul at Hamburg under the name of Baron de Hohenberg. Under that name I landed at New Orleans but having been since known by real name of Prince Frederick Paul Guillaume of Wurtemberg, cousin of the reigning king, I have no further motives for keeping incognito and that it might be a pledge of the sincerity of my motives I seal this my request with my princely seal."

It may have been this business of traveling incognito, or trying to—he was recognized by a fellow traveler on the steamboat—that led to official suspicion that the Prince really was spying out the country with the idea of setting up a German colony somewhere in North America or maybe establishing a German company to get into the fur trade. Although his subsequent actions never gave any support to either idea, it lasted for years. In 1851, Father Pierre-Jean de Smit, the traveling Jesuit missionary, met up with the Prince on the Platte river and reported hearing the same rumors, although, he said, he had no knowledge whether they were true. De Smit said that later he learned that the Prince was looking for a location that would be good farming country, "for the purpose of founding a German colony."

Two weeks later Clark told John C. Calhoun, who was Secretary of War, that he'd given the passport to the Prince and then made one of his rare misjudgments of a man. "This Gentleman (or Prince as he may be termed) has set out to the Council Bluffs in a Boat of one of our traders;" he wrote, "and as I very much suspect will neither have inclination nor perseverance to go on much further. He is fond of Killing Birds and collecting plants which appearrs to be of greatest pleasure to him.

"As to political, or any other Talents which he may possess I can say but little, as they appear to be very limited."

In fact, the Prince had both inclination and perseverance: he eventually made five trips to America, travelling over much of the west, and on this first trip spent five months visiting forts and Indian tribes; on another he spent the winter living with the Sioux.

Despite Clark's reservations, he invited the Prince to come out to his farm, where a delegation of Pottawatomies were to call. Led by their chief, Stream of the Rock, they spent a half hour discussing their grievances and passing the peace pipe. At the conclusion, the chief shook hands with Clark, with Major Benjamin O'Fallon, an Indian agent, and with the Prince. Later, in a trader's office, the Prince had a drink with the chief.

Clark must have mentioned Baptiste Charbonneau to the Prince because a month later travelling up the Missouri the Prince made a stop at a small trading settlement of creoles and half breeds near the mouth of the Kansas River and there met the seventeen-year-old son of Sacagawea and Toussaint Charbonneau; the Prince knew who he was.

Prince Paul proceeded on his tour inland, travelling as far as Fort Recovery, six hundred miles up the Missouri (near present Chamberlain, South Dakota). Near Fort Recovery, a trading post, he met Toussaint Charbonneau, who was there as an interpreter; his journal gives no indication that he was aware that Toussaint was Baptiste's father. The Prince would hire him on his next trip to America. Returning, on October 9, 1823, five months after he had headed into the wilderness, his boat stopped at the Kansas and picked up the half-Indian boy.

Baptiste Charbonneau's European adventure was about to begin.

On November 3, the Prince and Baptiste went aboard the steamboat Cincinnati, bound for New Orleans. The boat was heavily loaded with lead and because of low water in the first two days it ran aground several times, although got free. A day later "a terrific impact startled everybody," the Prince wrote. "The cry: 'The boat is sinking.'" The Cincinnati had hit a snag and the bottom had been holed. There was a great uproar; "With remarkable presence of mind and the greatest courage the captain and the engineer tried to restore order among the passengers who ran about in great confusion."

The pilot was able to run the boat into shallow water near the bank and the crew got all the passengers ashore, along with their baggage. "This was extremely fortunate, for in the prevailing cold and the stormy weather only a few could have saved themselves by swimming." The Prince lost a few of his belongings and everything was soaked.

In his journal of his first trip to America the Prince noted that seven years later, at almost the same spot, the new steamboat New Jersey on which he was a passenger sank under the same circumstances. Life on the Mississippi, as Mark Twain would so famously record later, was hazardous.

The Prince and Baptiste put up with people of the town of St. Genevieve, which was near where the boat sank, and then returned to St. Louis by hired wagon. Finally, on December 5, they went aboard the steamboat Mandan, which had been put into service to take the stranded Cincinnati passengers, and started to New Orleans again, arriving December 19.

Five days later the travelers boarded the brig Smyrna bound for Europe. (Prince Paul bought the tickets with a promissory note, according to one historian, and it was eighteen months before it was paid). The trip was not a pleasure cruise. The winds failed, and the ship drifted on the waters of the Mississippi for two weeks. Someone on the ship wounded an alligator, which was hauled aboard and put in a barrel, where it arrived, still alive, in France. The Prince petulently noted that because of the delay "My patience was put to a severe test."

Finally, on January 7, the wind came up and the Smyrna reached the sea and "quickly left the land behind."

The Prince waxed philosophical. He praised the people, high and low, he'd met on his journey; they'd been friendly and helpful.

"A feeling of deep emotion overcame me as the last bit of land was lost from sight...." "I was filled with respect for many institutions of these states. They are approaching a higher development and destiny with giant strides. My wishes certainly go out to my American friends, that the wise laws of the nation, which are founded on reason, may remain unchanged by innovations, as a memorial to the venerable founders, and that the great philanthropic work may go unhindered."

That is a proposition that has been debated ever since he wrote.

Toward the end of January the ship was caught in a storm. The rolling "became unbearable." Waves washed over the deck, carrying away some of the railing, water barrels and other gear stored on deck. The temperature dropped to fourteen degrees with hail and snow. The fury lasted for two weeks. Fortunately when the ship reached the English channel the weather was moderate, and on January 14, 1824, it docked at Havre de Grace, France.

Baptiste Charbonneau, half Indian, almost nineteen years old, had arrived in the Old World, where he was to spend the next six years.

Unfortunately, not much is known about his years with the Prince. Although the latter kept journals of all five trips to America, none has been found for the European years 1824 to 1829, the period that Baptiste was there. Considering that he was a man who kept extensive accounts of his travels this is an inexplicable, and regrettable, gap.

Ann W. Hafen, in her sketch of Baptiste in the collection called *The Mountain Men,* says the Prince and he went hunting in the Black Forest and the Prince referred to Baptiste as his "hunter extraordinary;" the source is unknown. Historian Hebard reported that in 1927 an American minister visiting Stuttgart saw in a school hall an oil painting titled "Prince Paul and his Indian boy." But it's never been seen again.

The Prince recalled the time with Baptiste in a journal of his fourth tour, some twenty-five years later. He was visiting John Sutter, known as the "King of California," on his vast farm on the American River where he lived in "a veritable castle"—a building of which the Prince was very familiar, since he lived in one himself—in 1850 and watching a group of Indians, including some Snakes, thresh wheat by driving their horses over it. "Among these latter was a handsome youth who reminded me, on account of his startling likeness, of a lad from the same tribe whom I took to Europe with me from a fur-trading post at the mouth of the Kansas, in western Mississippi, in the fall of 1823, and who was my companion there on all my travels over Europe and northern Africa until 1829, when he returned with me to America in 1829."

At least that's one translation of the Prince's comments. Another is less elaborate: "One of these Snake Indians was a very bright fellow and reminded me of B. Charboneau who followed me to Europe in 1823 and whose mother was Scho-sho-ne."

In either case, this is the only mention of Baptiste's years in Europe that was found until recently. In 1998 a book by Robert L. Dyer and Hans von Sachsen-Altenburg called *Duke Paul of Wurttemberg on the Missouri Frontier: 1823, 1830 and 1851* added a few details. Sachsen-Altenburg, a German, said that after the fall of the Berlin Wall he was able to conduct research in archives and libraries previously "unreachable." Parts of the book are based on records "not thought to have existed or survived," Sachsen-Altenburg wrote; many were believed destroyed in a World War II bombing raid in 1945. But in those and others he ran across references to Prince Paul and "an Indian," and pursuing further found more information. After Prince Paul and Baptiste arrived in Germany, he wrote, "the two young men embarked upon the traditional circuit expected of a prince who wanted to see and to be seen. The long distance between Stuttgart and Carlsruhe allowed visits to many castles." And, the author indicated, when Prince Paul married a Bavarian Princess, Sophie von Turn und Taxis, in 1827, Baptiste was present at a four-hundred-plate seating that "exceeded anything ever seen before in the castle." When the reigning king assigned the enormous castle at Mergentheim to the Prince, Baptiste moved there with him and his bride.

A Stuttgart researcher, Monika Filas, in 1999 reported more intriguing information. Exploring the life of a Mexican who lived in Prince Paul's household starting in 1831, she had the Bad Mergentheim parish records searched and discovered that Baptiste apparently had fathered a child while in Germany. Recorded was the birth of Anton Fries on February 20, 1829 and his death the following May 15. According to the records the baby was the son of "Johann Baptist Charbonnau of St. Louis 'called the American' in the service of Duke Paul of this place and Anastasia Katharina Fries, unmarried daughter of the late Georg Fries, a soldier here." (Translation by Albert Furtwangler of Salem, Oregon, who found Firla's research in a German publication).

Firla learned that the Mexican, one Juan Alvardo, died at Mergentheim in 1841 and among his possessions were schoolbooks in geography, history, arthmetic, French and Spanish, indicating that the Prince was seeing to the education of his young ward. This would suggest he earlier had done the same for Baptiste.

Baptiste's relationship with the Prince has been the subject of some debate by historians: Was he a companion or a servant? The only conclusion that can be made from the brief references that the Prince made to the young man is that his role probably was some of both.

The Prince's marriage failed, and he decided to go back to America, taking Baptiste with him.

The return trip started in May, 1829, from Bremen; it is unknown whether this was before or after the death of Charbonneau's child. From there the travelers went to Bordeaux, with a side trip to Madrid. From Bordeaux to three months in Santa Domingo, and from there to New Orleans and on to St. Louis, arriving December 1.

The Prince received another passport from Clark and headed back up the Missouri.; apparently he left Baptiste in St. Louis. On this second trip to the West, he again hired Toussaint Charbonneau as a translator.

Baptiste's life as a mountain man was about to begin.

5

LIFE AS A MOUNTAIN MAN

In February, 1830, the American Fur Company, John Jacob Astor's outfit, which by negotiation, browbeating, sharp practices and hard work had taken over much of the fur business in the Missouri Valley, sent from St. Louis its first expedition to the Rocky Mountains. Its goal was to wrest control of the fur trade there away from the Rocky Mountain Fur Company. Baptiste Charbonneau was a member of that party.

Also a member was Warren A. Ferris of Buffalo, New York. Ferris had left home at 18; he said it was because his mother objected to his pipe smoking. His stepfather was a surveyor and Ferris trained in the same profession. That training later stood him in good order because when he later moved to Texas he was appointed surveyor and laid out much of what became the city of Dallas. He also engaged in land speculation, which probably was illegal considering his position and also turned out to be only marginally profitable. Also as it turned out, Ferris was among the better writers of the many traders, trappers and tourists who kept journals or wrote memoirs of their travels.

He gave a tongue-in-cheek explanation of why people like himself joined the company. "The party consists of some thirty men, mostly Canadians," he wrote, "but a few there are, like myself, from various parts of the Union. Each has some plausible excuse for joining, and the aggregate of disinteredness would delight the most ghostly saint in the Roman calender. Engage for money! no, not they;– –health, and the strong desire of seeing strange lands, of beholding nature in the savage grandeur of her primeval state,—these are the only arguments that *could* have persuaded such independent and high-minded young fellows to adventure with the American Fur Company in a trip to the mountain wilds of the great west. But they are active, vigorous, resolute, daring and such are the kind of men the service requires. The Company have no reason to be dissatisfied, nor have they. Everything *promises* well. No doubt there will be two fortunes apiece for us. Westward! Ho!"

Others had a less romantic view. The trapper Zenas Leonard, writing about his companions, said that some of them were men wanted by the law. "Many were anxious to return to the States, but feared to do so, lest the offended law might hold them responsible for misdemeanors committed previous to their embarking in the trapping business." But, he added, "Others could not be persuaded to do so for any price—declaring that civilized life had no charms for them." Most were simply aspiring capitalists, hoping to get rich. A few did.

By late autumn, Baptiste's company was encamped for the winter in the Cache Valley, near the present Hyrum, Utah, then moved south to Ogden's Hole, at what is now Huntsville, Utah. In April of 1831, the company split, with one group under Lucien Fontenelle, to which Ferris was attached, another under the command of Joseph Robidoux and a third under Andrew Drips. All were experienced mountain men. Baptiste joined Robidoux.

Robidoux's party traveled north, and then down the Snake river to the Portneuf (which enters the Snake near the present Pocatello, Idaho) and then moved on to present American Falls. There it divided again, with one group trapping the Wind River while the other, which included a man named J.H. Stevens, moved toward the Malade River (now called the Big Wood).

Stevens told Ferris what happened:

The small party traveled through a lava field that spread for forty or fifty miles. Except for a couple who had filled beaver skins, the men were without water and because they'd been eating dried buffalo meat, "which is alone sufficient to engender the most maddening desire for water," were suffering. After stopping for a couple of hours because it was too dark to find their way, the moon rose and the party marched and rode the rest of the night and into the day, which was hot. "Some of the party had recourse to the last expedient to mitigate their excessive thirst, and others ate powder, chewed bullets, etc., but all to no purpose." Orders were given that it was every man for himself. One turned his horse from northwest, the way they'd been heading, and pointed northeast, saying anyone who followed would be led to water by nightfall.

Everyone did.

"Our suffering became more and more intense, and our poor animals, oppressed with heat and toil, and parching with thirst, now began to give out, and were left by the way side. Several of our poor fellows were thus deprived of their horses, and although almost speechless and scarcely able to stand, were compelled to totter along on foot. Many of our packed mules, unable to proceed any further, sank down and were left with their parched tongues protruding from their mouths. Some of the men, too, dropped down totally exhausted, and were left, beseeching their companions to hasten on, and return to them with water, if they should be so fortunate as to succeed in reaching it."

Finally, one of the men who had gone ahead, fired off his gun, and the men––and even the animals—knew what it meant. Water had been sighted, four miles ahead. They reached it at sunset, "and man and beast, regardless of depth, plunged, and drank, and laved, and drank again."

And vomited from all the water.

They spent the night and the following morning carrying water back to the spent men and animals and got them all to the riverside camp.

Except for Baptiste Charbonneau, "who could nowhere be found, and was supposed to have wandered from the trail and perished."

The party moved on. Reaching the Malade, they learned why it was so named: Despite having heard stories of another group of trappers that had become seriously ill from eating beavers from this river, they did it themselves, with the same result. It is the only river mentioned by trappers that held beaver that somehow were poisonous to man.

The party eventually returned to the Cache Valley via the Porteneuf, where they found Drips and his party—and Baptiste Charbonneau.

Baptiste said he'd lost the trail, but reached the Malade after dark where he discovered a village of Indians. Fearing they were unfriendly, he decided to retrace his steps and find the main company. He filled a beaver skin with water and set off—and wandered for eleven days "during which he suffered a good deal from hunger" before finding the company.

As it turned out, the "Indian village" Baptiste had seen was a camp of trappers of the Hudson Bay Company, and his own camp was only a short distance below it. "But his unluky star was in the ascendant, and it cost him eleven day's toil, danger, and privation to find friends."

That's the last mention of Baptiste on this trip. Warren Ferris spent six years in the mountains before returning to St. Louis. He never went back to the Rockies, moving instead to the Southwest.

Later that year Baptiste met up with one of the legendary mountain men, Joe Meek. Meek, a nineteen-year-old greenhorn, had signed on with William Sublette's fur company in St. Louis and headed west. The company trapped the Missouri and Yellowstone and holed up for the winter in the Powder River valley of what now is Wyoming. During the winter Meek was dispatched to take messages to company headquarters in St. Louis. He travelled with a French-Canadian named Legarde, who was captured by Pawnee Indians. Meek avoided capture and traveled on alone for several days until he met up with a party of traders and trappers that was headed to St. Louis, turned over his dispatches to them and headed back to the Powder river. With him on the return trip was Baptiste, who apparently had been with the St.Louis-bound party.

By 1833 Baptiste was working for another of the great mountain men, Jim Bridger. Bridger was a principal in the Rocky Mountain Fur Company, the most famous of all the companies that trapped the Rockies. Another great mountain man, Thomas Fitzpatrick, also was a principal, the head of the operation. He was, next to Kit Carson, the most famous of the group of trappers, traders, guides and explorers that roamed the west.

Bridger's brigade traveled to the summer rendezvous, which this year was held in the valley of the upper Green River. William Ashley, former lieutenant governor of Missouri and later Congressman, had devised the rendezvous in 1825 and it became an annual event. Before then, a trapper spent a year collecting his beaver pelts and then had to trek to St. Louis to sell them—more likely exchange them—for the goods to keep going another year. Or he could sell them, at cut-rate prices, to traders at the posts that sprang up along the Missouri and Platte rivers.

Under Ashley's scheme, a supply train, at first pack horses and mules and later wagons, was sent out from St. Louis to a pre-arranged location in the mountains where the trappers—who knew the location from what was called the mountain telegraph, that is, word of mouth—were waiting. This arrangement let the trappers stay in the mountains the year around. And it made Ashley, who supplied the trains at a handsome markup, rich.

Everybody showed up at these fur fairs. Trapper Osborne Russell described one of the gatherings. "Here presented what might be termed a mixed multitude the whites were chiefly American and Canadian French with some Dutch, Scotch, Irish, English, halfbreed, and full blood Indians of nearly every tribe in the Rocky Mountains. Some were gambling at Cards some playing the Indians game of hand and others horse racing while here and there could be seen small groups collected under shady trees relating the events of the past year."

There also were pliant Indian girls and liquor (even though Congress in 1832 outlawed alcohol in Indian country) and as a result of the latter, occasional shootings. It was wild. One visitor called it "a perfect bedlam." The writer Washington Irving described it as "Saturnalia among the mountains." Bernard DeVoto called rendezvous "the mountain man's Christmas, county fair, harvest festival, and crowned-slave carnival of Saturn." Nathaniel Wyeth, a straitlaced New Englander, wasn't amused. After looking over the crowd at the 1832 gathering, he called it "a great majority of scoundrels."

Rendezvous moved the goods.

Osborne Russell said that he paid $2 a pound for coffee, sugar and tobacco, $4 a pint for alcohol, $20 for a blanket and $5 for a cotton shirt. He claimed the trappers were paying a two thousand per cent markup over the cost of the goods at St. Louis. According to Nathaniel Wyeth, a good hunter was paid $400 a year, payable in goods marked up six hundred per cent. The traders charged Indians even higher prices. Thus it is no surprise that the people who got rich in the fur trade were those running the supply houses—Ashley, who supposedly took out $50,000 to $80,000; William Sublette, and, of course, John Jacob Astor.

The 1833 rendezvous was a big one, probaby the biggest ever held; Bridger, Fitzpatrick, William and Milton Sublette, Capt. Benjamin Bonneville with his company, Nathaniel Wyeth with his. Wyeth said there were two hundred and fifty whites at the fair and a thousand or more Indians. And who should show up, along with the regulars, but a Scotch aristocrat and adventurer, Sir William Drummond Stewart, with a large personal party. In one of those coincidences that regularly seemed to occur in the fur trade, ten years later Baptiste would be on an expedition with Stewart. Also at the fur fair was Benjamin Harrison, son of General—and future President—William Henry Harrison. Young Harrison, who had a drinking problem, had been sent west to dry out, an unlikely venue to cure alcoholism.

The most excitement at this rendezvous was a rabid wolf or wolves; twelve men were bitten and so were horses and oxen. Their bellowing terrified the campers. One or two men may have died. The wolf escaped. Joe Meek, who also was there, wasn't bitten. He said he was so drunk that if he had been bitten, it would have either killed the wolf or cured him.

Some historians say Baptiste was with Bridger in 1832, but evidence of that is inconclusive. So whether he attended the most famous rendezvous of all, the one held that year at Pierre's Hole, a beautiful valley at the western foot of the Three Tetons, isn't clear. The area now is called the Teton Basin and is in Teton County, Idaho. At the eastern foot is Jackson's Hole.

As that rendezvous was breaking up a brigade of trappers heading out ran into a band of Gros Ventres. The Indians sent a chief forward for a parley. Antonie Godin, whose father had been killed by Blackfeet, and a Flathead Indian went to meet him. When the Indian raised the peace pipe, Godin grabbed his hand, the

Flathead shot the chief, Godin grabbed the Indian's blanket and the two raced back to camp.

That set off a battle that lasted until the next day. The Gros Ventres retreated into a thicket and started building fortifications. After reinforcements arrived from the rendezvous, the whites attempted to charge the barricades; one white was killed almost instantly and William Sublette was shot in the shoulder. After daylong skirmishing, the fight ended with nightfall. The next morning the whites discovered the Gros Ventres had slipped away. Final count was three whites killed, four or five wounded, eight of their Nez Perce and Flathead allies killed or wounded. The Gros Ventres later said they'd had twenty-six men killed.

It was known forever after as The Battle of Pierre's Hole. And no rendezvous was held there again.

After the 1833 rendezvous, Wyeth, a New Englander who was trying to become a fur-trading mogul, with no success, went trapping on the Popo Agie; Bridger's outfit was in the vicinty and he sent four men to look for Wyeth. The four were Baptiste, Thompson, Smith and Evans and they ran into trouble. A roving band of about fifteen Shoshone showed up and had what appeared a friendly smoke. A day or so later, however, they showed up again, this time to steal the party's horses. Thompson, who was supposed to be guarding them while the others were out hunting, was asleep.

Wyeth recorded what happened:

"He was waked by a noise among the horses which he supposed to [be] his comrades come to water them raising his head and opening his eyes the first thing that presented itself to his sight was the muzzle of a gun in the hands of an Indian it was immediately discharged and so near his head that the front piece of his cap alone saved his eyes from being put out by the powder the Ball entered the head outside of the eye and breaking the cheek bone passed downward and lodged

68

behind the ear in the neck this stunned him and while insensible an arrow was shot into him on top of the shoulder downward which entered about 6 inches."

Wyeth then commented, "The Inds. got 7 horses all there were. charboneau pursued them on foot but wet his gun in crossing a little stream and only snapped twice."

Thompson, remarkably enough, was patched up and survived.

By 1834, the beaver in the usually productive areas of the Rockies were nearly trapped out, forcing the trappers to range further and further, including into the always dangerous territory of the Blackfeet. At the same time, John Jacob Astor, who had gotten rich spotting trends, noticed that in Europe, where he spent a lot of his time, "they now make hats of silk in place of beaver." So he sold the American Fur Co. His timing was nearly perfect. In 1832 beaver skins were selling as high as six dollars a pound. By 1840, the price was one dollar.

And the Rocky Mountain Fur Company disintegrated. Two of its partners sold out and after a brief spell under Fitzpatrick, Milton Sublette and Jim Bridger, the company dissolved. Bridger and Fitzpatrick went to work for their old, bitter competitor, the American Fur Co.

There was a terrible irony in this. The previous year after the rendezvous Fitzpatrick and his men had set out for the valley of Tongue River where he expected to find the Crows and get permission to trap in their country. Instead, "Before I had time for form or ceremony of any kind, they robbed me and my men of everything we possessed." Fitzpatrick charged that the American Fur Co. had instigated the attack, and the Indians later admitted it. The final bone in the throat was that Kenneth McKenzie, American Fur's head trader, offered to sell Fitzpatrick's beaver skins that had been taken by the Indians and were clearly marked R.M.F. Co., *back* to him.

But business is business.

Under a variety of corporate arrangements, the Rocky Mountain Fur Co. had lasted twelve years. Fur trade historian Hiram Chittenden estimated that during that period it shipped upwards of a thousand packs of beaver pelts, one hundred pounds to the pack—that amounted to fifty to one hundred pelts—worth $500,000, to St. Louis.

William Marshall Anderson, who had gone to the Rockies with William Sublette, met up with Baptiste in June of 1834, when the latter was trapping with Fitzpatrick. In his *Rocky Mountain Journals,* Anderson recalls that one night there was a mock war dance ""in compliment, I believe, to me" and Baptiste "was the principal actor in this scene." Anderson went on to comment that "Of him there is something whispered which makes him an object of interest to me. At all events he is an intelligent and interesting young man. He converses fluently & well in English, reading & writing & speaking with ease French and German—understan{din}g several of the Indian dialects—."

In August of that same year Anderson recorded another incident involving Baptiste. Still in camp with Fitzpatrick, who had joined with the American Fur Company camp, Anderson reported rather casually in his *Journal* that "A stabbing match took place, which had like to have produced serious disturbances in both camps. Last night horses were cut loose and halters were stolen, which led this morning to the charges and recriminations that produced the difficulty—Charbonneauu accused a young white fellow whom he had discovered prowling about in the night with having committed the theft—for which compliment he {the white man} was kind enough to offer Baptiste a flogging—not choosing it, and being somewhat liberally inclined he lent the accused his butcher-knife up to the hilt in the muscles of his shoulder—." That apparently ended that dispute, without further trouble.

Baptiste then disappeared from notice until Willard Smith recorded him in 1839 as working as a hunter for a party headed by Andrew Sublette and Louis Vasquez that left Independence, Missouri, for their post, Fort Vasquez, on the upper South Platte, near the present Platteville, Colorado. Vasquez first went up the Missouri in 1823 and worked the far western trade for more than thirty years. He later became a partner with Jim Bridger in the ownership of Fort Bridger in the southwestern corner of Wyoming. Andrew Sublette, who had four brothers, all in the fur trade, spent a decade in the trade and in 1844 was captain of a caravan over the Oregon Trail. Sublette moved to California after gold was discovered and in 1853 was killed by a grizzly.

The August, 1839 Sublette-Vasquez party consisted of thirty-two people with four wagons loaded with goods for the Indian trade, each drawn by six mules. The drivers rode the wagons, the rest of the company of French-Canadians, Americans, Spanish and half breeds, rode mules.

Mountain men generally favored mules over horses for use in the mountains, although they also liked to have a couple of fast horses to chase buffalo on the hunts. Mules could carry bigger loads farther than horses, and the trappers swore that mules were far more sensitive to the presence of Indians, snorting and raising their ears when there were skulkers. And, when supplies ran out, a mule was better eating than a horse. But buffalo was the first choice of food. William Ashley commented that "nothing...is actually necessary for the support of men in the wilderness than a plentiful supply of good fresh meat." That was buffalo, preferably fat cows or calves, followed by mountain sheep, deer, elk, mule, horse and dog.

The early part of the trip was easy enough. The company followed the Santa Fe Trail for four hundred miles, then along the Arkansas River to Bent's Fort, more than five hundred miles from Independence. About three hundred miles out from Independence, there were incredible herds of buffalo. In late August Smith recorded "Towards evening we passed a great number of buffaloes, the prairie being actually alive with them. They extended probably about four miles, and numbered nearly two hundred thousand." If that was exaggerated, there's no question there were a lot.

The buffalo herds once were in the millions and roamed as far east as the present site of Washington D.C.; by 1890 there were less than one thousand left, according to David J. Wishart, in *The Fur Trade of the American West.* By 1840, he said, buffalo were no longer found west of the Rockies because of hunting by trappers and the Indians. Even so, he quoted one trader working east of the Rockies as saying in 1854 that "Buffalo are very numerous and we do not, after 20 years experience, find that they decrease in this quarter, although upward of 150,000 are killed annually throughout the extent of our trade."

But despite the killing by the traders and the Indians, who killed to get the hides to trade for the goods offered by the traders, it wasn't until the coming of the railroads that the real slaughter began; easy access for hide hunters and sportsmen made the killing easy. In 1872 half a million buffalo were killed for their hides; in 1873 three-quarters of a million hides went east on three western railroads. Author Dan E. Clark, in his 1937 book *The West in American History,* recorded that there was a stack of buffalo bones twelve feet high and a half a mile long beside the Santa Fe railroad tracks.

The Sublette-Vasquez party killed some buffalo, but not without trouble; the animals were hard to bring down and dangerous when wounded, and the prairie was dotted with holes from prairie dog colonies. Several of the hunters were severely injured when they were thrown after their horses stepped in the holes.

There was another way to kill buffalo, Smith wrote, called approaching. The hunter put on a white blanket coat and a white cap, "so as to resemble a white wolf as much as possible," and crawled on his hands and knees toward the buffalo until he got within 150 yards, then sank his knife in the ground, rested his gun on the knife and fired. It usually took more than one shot, even if the buffalo was shot through the heart, he said.

But the men enjoyed the excitement of chasing the buffalo on horseback despite the dangers. "It is a fine sight to see them *running* the herd."

A ten-day march from Bent's Fort put the party at Fort St. Vrain, where there were a number of free trappers. After three days during which "The men at the fort have been carousing, etc., having got drunk on alcohol," a party of eight men, including Baptiste, two squaws and three children, continued west over the Rockies to Brown's Hole on the Green River, where they planned to make winter quarters, trapping beaver until the weather got too bad. Other trappers, including Kit Carson, already were there. Historian Chrittenden described Brown's Hole "as little less than a solitary mountain prison, surrounded with the grandest scenes of nature, but cut off entirely from the outside world."

But a peaceful winter at Brown's Hole was not to be. There was serious Indian trouble. A few days before arriving at Brown's Hole the party had passed where it appeared there had been a fight between whites and Indians. Kit Carson filled them in. A party of seven whites and two squaws had come there from Brown's Hole to kill buffalo and dry the meat and was attacked by about twenty Sioux, who killed one white. After exchanging shots, a chief rode towards them and made offers of peace. A white went out and talked the chief and several others into coming forward. When the Indians advanced, the whites killed the chief. The remaining Indians fled, but didn't forget. On November 1, Sioux stole one hundred and fifty horses from the trappers. And in late January, the trappers somehow got word that the Sioux whose chief had been killed were coming back in the spring with the whole tribe for revenge.

That's when the enjoyable part of the expedition ended. On January 24, the Vasquez party decided to head back to Fort Vasquez for safety, even though it meant crossing the mountains in winter. The weather had, after all, been mild. So a party of twenty, including fourteen men, Baptiste among them, four squaws and two children started out. Three days later two feet of snow fell. Within a week the snow was six feet deep. By the middle of February provisions were running out and there were no buffalo. They started out with thirty-nine horses and mules. Now the animals were dying daily from lack of food and water. The party ate the horses as they died. All but two did. On February 24 the hunters were able to kill three buffalo, "which was the first fat meat we had seen for twenty days." They still were one hundred and fifty miles from the fort. Smith and two others started for the fort to get help, but couldn't make it and returned to the party. Four days after they returned a trapper named Biggs and a half breed started for the fort by a different route, taking a horse to carry their provisions. Forty-two days later he and Vasquez returned, with enough horses to carry their furs (which had been cached several days back) but not enough to ride.

On April 24—three months after they set out—the party arrived safely at Fort Vasquez.

Smith was a graduate of Rensselaar Polytechnic Institute and he'd been given the trip as a graduation present by his father. As a college graduate he should have known bettter, but nevertheless he identified Baptiste as "a son of Capt. Clarke the great Western traveller, and a companion of Lewis—he had received an education, in Europe, during seven years." In one sentence he had two mistakes, misspelling Clark's name and Baptiste's paternity.

That Baptiste wasn't Clark's son is certain. Clark and Lewis arrived at the Mandan villages in October of 1804, Sacagawea gave birth the following February. That Toussaint Charbonneau was the father is almost as certain. The Indian girl had been his slave and wife for five or six years. But it wasn't the only time that Clark's name had been linked sexually with Sacagawea with no foundation except that he obviously was fond of her as well as her son. Among the Nez Perce who, led by the famous Chief Joseph, fought U.S. troops in 1877, was an old Indian named Tzi-kal-tza; tribal lore was that he was the son of William Clark, although obviously not by Sacagawea. Even longer lasting was the rumor that Lewis had a child by her. The great western historian Bernard DeVoto, writing in 1946, noted that "Working desultorily on Lewis and Clark for some years, I have encountered that legend in odd places and have corresponded with a man who claims to belong to the line so founded. This sort of thing can never be proved or disproved. I have never seen any evidence whatever of any kind..."

The rumors may have been fed by the fact that early in the expedition Lewis and Clark shared sleeping quarters with Sacagawea in a large buffalo-skin tepee. But in the same lodge slept her husband, the baby, and George Druillard.

A lack of facts didn't stop writers and movie makers from creating a romance between Sacagawea and Clark. A popular paperback novel by Anna Lee Waldo, *Sacajawea,* published in 1979, featured what Lewis and Clark scholar Arlen J. Large called "a heavy-breathing love affair between Clark and Sacagawea." Even more bizarre, in 1955 a movie called *The Far Horizon,* starring Charlton Heston as Clark, Fred MacMurry as Lewis and Donna Reed, of all people, as the Indian girl Sacagawea, included a fight between Lewis and Clark over the latter's plan to marry the (married) girl.

All wonderful nonsense. There may well have been affection between Clark and Sacagawea. But no romance, let alone a fight between the two Captains. If such a thing had happened, it wouldn't be surprising that it wasn't recorded in their journals. But to think that the soldiers who kept diaries, Patrick Gass, Joseph

Whitehead and John Ordway, would ignore such a significant event in *their* journals is beyond reason.

Claims that Lewis or Clark conceived a child with some Indian woman while on the Expedition have existed almost from the time they returned to St. Louis. In St. Alban Cemetery at Fort Hale, S.D., is a granite gravestone on which is inscribed "Joseph Lewis, 'DeSmet,' 1805-1889, son of Meriwether Lewis of the Famed Lewis & Clark Expedition." Fort Hale is near where the Expedition camped on September 16-17, 1804, on its way west. It may have been a descendant of DeSmet, also spelled DeSomet and DeSomit, who wrote DeVoto. His mother supposedly was a Sioux. But there is absolutely no evidence that such a liason with Lewis took place and only claims by the DeSmet (DeSomet, DeSomit) family to support it.

The Vasquez-Sublette partnership didn't do well. Two days after the Vasquez trapping party arrived back at Fort Vasquez, seven men, including Baptiste and Smith, pushed off a thirty-six-foot boat and set off down the Platte headed for St. Louis carrying their entire season's take—seven hundred buffalo robes and four hundred buffalo tongues. The same year the Bent, St. Vrain outfit brought down *fifteen thousand* robes and "considerable furs"—some twenty times their rivals' production.

Smith reported that, as usual when their boat tied up for the night, Baptiste "went out a short distance from the river to shoot a buffalo for his meat."

About then Smith realized that *he'd* never killed a buffalo. He quickly learned that the buffalo's reputation for ferocity and the difficulty of killing one weren't exaggerated. Smith had broken his rifle and was carrying what he called a fusee, or short gun. This was a smooth-bored flintlock shortened for ease of handling on horseback. The Hudson's Bay Company traded them in large numbers to the

Indians, probably because they were so inferior in range and accuracy to the rifled gun used by the trappers that it put the Indians at a great disadvantage.

Smith spotted a buffalo and started after it on foot. The buffalo spotted him, and started running, uphill. Smith followed and after a mile-and-a-half run the buffalo stopped to rest and graze with some others. Smith managed to get within fifty feet of him, kneeled down, rested his rifle on a ramrod and fired at the buffalo's heart. The ball struck and the buffalo charged; Smith got away. He loaded another shot and fired again. The buffalo again charged and Smith again got away. He loaded again, using the last of his powder. Again the ball hit, and again the buffalo charged—but badly weakened, then laid down. Smith, without powder, then took a six-inch butcher knife he was carrying and crawling up to the wounded animal tried to cut his hamstrings to disable him. "I had no sooner cut through the thick skin of his leg when smarting with pain the infuriated animal arose and plunged at me and would probably have killed me if it had not been for the miraculous arrival of our bull dog Turk." The dog grabbed the buffalo by the nose. Smith shook his powder horn and got enough for half a charge, stuck the muzzle into the buffalo's mouth and fired down his throat. For good measure, Smith stabbed him several times in the heart. With the dog holding off a "large circle of white wolves," Smith cut out the tongue and part of the meat and hiked back to the boat.

The party arrived at St. Louis July 3, eleven months after it had left it, "having come two thousand miles from the mountains in sixty-nine days," and that ended Smith's infatuation with the mountains.

The Vasquez-Sublette partnership broke up and a little later George Frederick Ruxton, an English adventurer who had resigned his commission in the British army, placed Baptiste again at a winter rendezvous at Brown's Hole, now known as Brown Park. Ruxton wrote that "Here were soon congregated many mountaineers, whose names are famous in the history of the Far West. Fitzpatrick and Hatcher, and old Bill Williams, well-known leaders of trapping parties, soon arrived with their bands. Sublette came in with his men from Yellow Stone, and many of Wyeth's New Englanders were there. Chabonard with his half-breeds, Wah-keitchas all, brought his peltries from the lower country…"

French-Canadians were called wah-keitchas—bad medicine—by the Indians, who said they were treacherous and vindictive. Ruxton's comment indicates Baptiste had been running a trapping brigade in the southwest. Earlier Ruxton quoted an unnamed trapper as remarking that at one rendezvous Baptiste and trapper Bill Garey sat in camp "for twenty hours at a deck of euker. Them was Bent's Indian traders up on Arkansa."

6

A PARTY OF SWELLS

By 1842 Baptiste was working for the trading company Bent & St. Vrain—and stuck on an island in the Platte.

Charles and William Bent, brothers from St. Louis, and Ceran St. Vrain had a trading post on the South Platte they called Fort St. Vrain and Baptiste was dispatched from there as the head of a mostly Mexican crew to carry furs down the river to St. Louis in boats that had been built at the fort. The Platte was low, and the trip was a nightmare; the boats had to be pushed and dragged over shallows. At one point they unloaded the furs and carried them over shallows to the next patch of floatable water.

Baptiste finally gave up forty miles downstream from the fort and set up camp on an island that he named St. Helena, which was no accident and showed a sense of humor. St. Helena was the island in the South Atlantic Ocean to which Napolean Bonaparte was exiled in 1815 after his disaster at Waterloo, a fact that Baptiste prrobably picked up in his European travels with the Prince.

Baptiste and his crew spent the summer on the island and played the genial hosts to some distinguished visitors. One of them was Captain John Charles Fremont, who got the title The Pathfinder for his explorations of the West, although it was mostly Kit Carson who found the paths after Fremont had picked the implausible routes. Carson was Fremont's guide on this trip.

On July 9, Fremont recorded in his report to Congress, that "Mr. Chabonard was in the service of Bent and St. Vrain's company, and had left their fort some forty or fifty miles above, in the spring, with boats laden with the furs of the last year's trade. He had met the same fortune as the voyageurs on the North fork, and finding it impossible to proceed, had taken up his summer's residence on this island...."

Fremont's reference to the voyageurs on the North fork was to a party of fourteen men that sixty days earlier and three hundred miles upstream had left with barges loaded with American Fur Company furs. They had started well but soon ran into shallow water. They dragged and poled their boats, sometimes making only two or three miles. Finally they gave up, cached their furs, and packing their provisions on their backs, headed on foot to St. Louis.

Floating the Platte was no afternoon row on the lake.

It was a pleasant meeting with Baptiste, whom Fremont described as a "director" of Bent and St. Vrain. "Mr. C. received us hospitably," Fremont wrote. And Baptiste sent one of the crew out to gather mint, "with the aid of which he concocted very good julep, and some boiled buffalo tongue, and coffee with the luxury of sugar, soon were set before us."

A cocktail party on a sand bar in the South Platte!

Elsewhere, Fremont added to his comments about Baptiste. "Most of the men on the island were Mexicans, but the man in charge of the party was one Chabonard, a gentleman of excellent education and evidently a witty man, as he had named the little island on which the low water had imprisoned him St. Helena."

Just before he reached Baptiste's camp Fremont had run across Jim Beckwourth—or Beckwirth or Beckwerth, depending upon who was writing—one of the engaging rascals of the West. Beckwourth was out looking for a band of horses that had wandered off; the horses were "in charge of Mr. Chabonard." Fremont explained that the man he called Beckwith was a mulatto who had lived with the Crow Indians and "had risen to the rank of chief." When Fremont reached the camp he met Luisa Sandoval, a beautiful Spanish woman Beckwourth had recently married in Taos. Later, after one of Beckwourth's year-long trips to California to steal horses, he returned to find his lively wife had remarried in his absence. In his memoirs Beckwourth claimed she had thought he was dead, and begged him to take her back. But Beckwourth said he decided he liked the single life better, and instead bought a bar and store in Santa Fe.

He had a reputation as a very tough man, reckless and a thug and a liar. His eventual autobiography was replete with, at the very least, exaggerations. He and Baptiste would connect again in California.

Another visitor was Rufus Sage, twenty-five years old, who said he was prompted by "a love of adventure" and "an enfeebled state of health" to embark on the three years of travel that took him to California and Oregon and back. Also, he wanted to write a book.

Baptiste still was high and dry when Sage arrived at the end of August.

"The camp was under the direction of a half-breed, named Chabonard, who proved to be a gentleman of superior information," Sage wrote in his 1846 book *Rocky Mountain Life.* "He had acquired a classic education and could convese quite fluently in German, Spanish, French and English, as well as several Indian languages. His mind, also, was well stored with choice reading, and enriched by extensive travel and observation. Having visited most of the important places, both in England, France, and Germany, he knew how to turn his experience to good advangtage.

"There was a quaint humor and shrewdness in his conversation, so garbed with intelligence and perspicuity, that he at once insinuated himself into the good graces of listeners, and commanded their admiration and respect."

Strong praise that, with just a touch of white-man condescension, although one might wonder whether Baptiste hadn't been putting Sage on a bit.

In late May of 1843 Baptiste, having eventually gotten down the Platte, signed on in St. Louis as a mule-cart driver for William Sublette. Years later, William Clark Kennerly, who made the trip on which Baptiste drove the mule cart, said he was asked by the Historical Society of Wyoming, when a statue to Sacagawea was being erected, if Charbonneau spoke often of his mother and if he seemed to appreciate her fortitude and courage. "I regret to say that he spoke more often of the mules he was driving and might have been heard early and late expatiating in not too complimentary a manner on their stubborness."

Sublette was in charge of a party organized for one of the most interesting tourists ever to travel the West. He was Sir William Drummond Stewart, the Scotsman whom Baptiste had encountered ten years before at the rendezvous on the Green River.

Stewart had fought at Waterloo and had been mustered out of the British army as a captain. He had made his first trip to the United States in 1833 and spent six years roaming the west, some of it with yet another foreigner, Maximilian, Prince of Wied, who also had fought Napoleon, while in the Prussian army. Maximilian was in America to see the Indians.

Stewart quickly attracted attention from the lavish way he travelled. Before entering the rendezvous on that 1833 trip he donned a white leather jacket, a pair of trousers in green, royal blue, red and yellow, and wore a Panama hat. George Frederick Ruxton, an English adventurer who had resigned his commission in the British army, told of two hunters, down on their luck, meeting Stewart and his party at Independence Rock. The men, on foot, without powder and with broken rifles, were cooking rattlesnakes to eat after three starving days.

Stewart disdained the snakes, and had his cook prepare a huge meal from the hams, tongues, canned meat and other food carried in the wagons. That was topped off by horns of brandy. When they were finished, Stewart gave them powder, lead and flints and then presented them with two Indian ponies.

Ruxton's book, *Life in the Far West,* in which this story is told, is semi-fictional but accurate historically. So it may not be quite true, but does accurately describe the way Stewart travelled. Ruxton visited the United States twice, once taking leave when he was stationed with his regiment in Canada, and then again after his resignation; he was suspected of being an English spy. He died at twenty-eight in St. Louis, the result of injuries received when he fell from a mule onto a picket of a lodge that pierced his back.

There's no question that Stewart was generous. The artist Alfred Jacob Miller, traveling with Stewart, painted a picture at the 1837 rendezvous of Jim Bridger wearing a suit of armor that Stewart gave his friend, shipped over from Murthly Castle in Scotland.

On his second trip Stewart slept in a crimson tent, in which he burned incense. And July 4 he celebrated with his companions by serving roast beef and plum pudding and consuming twenty-four bottles of Rhine wine, along with juleps and hock.

The Stewart/Sublette party of 1843 was a motley one. William Sublette seemed a little bemused as he noted in his diary the makeup of his wards: "I took charge of the party of Some 60 men Sir William had 10 cartes & one Small 2 Mule Yankee

Waggon There was some 3 other Carts & one small 2 Horse Waggon Belonging to Individual gentlemen Some of the armey Some professional Gentlemen Some on the trip for pleasure Some for Health &c &c So we had doctors Lawyers Botanists Bugg Ketchers Hunters & men of nearly all professions &c &c One half or rather more was hired men Belonging to Sir William—which he had employed on the trip..."

It was a bunch of swells, out on a lark. And Sir William, who recently had sold a family estate in Scotland for $1,000,000 was footing much of the bill. He'd been so anxious to have John Audubon, the bird painter, come along he'd offered Audubon the use of five mules and a wagon, but Audubon declined.

Among the travelers, for adventure, were Jefferson Kennerly Clark, son of William Clark, whom Sir William had met on his first trip, and William Clark Kennerly, William Clark's nephew, who had grown up with Jeff Clark. Both were nineteen years old.

So Baptiste Charbonneau, who as an infant had traveled to the Pacific and back under the care of William Clark, now was heading west as one of the people taking care of Clark's son.

Sir William brought his Scotish valet, Corbie, and a boy servant. Kennerly had Cupid, his black servant.

Also along was Matthew Field, an assistant editor of the *New Orleans Picayune,* thirty-one, and a former actor, who also was getting a reputation as a writer and poet. He'd made one Western trip, to Santa Fe, and was anxious for another. But there was a complication: He had a wife and child and no income other than his newspaper earnings.

No problem; Stewart would pay his expenses and take care of his family.

Field, who thought the trip would be a "hunting frolic," filed regular dispatches, flowery ones, back to the *Picayune,* depending upon passing travelers for delivery.

He filled four notebooks with his observations for future pieces (he eventually published thirty-eight "sketches" in the *Picayune*) and his plans for a book.

"O, for the opportunity to branch out upon a *"Rocky Mountain Romance!"* he wrote in his diary."Give me only the *time*—I have all the *material*—and *I* can do it! (Mem) put *"Little Charboneau"* into verse."

"Little Charboneau" was thirty-eight years old then, but Field had been reading about the Lewis and Clark expedition at the time, when Baptiste *was* little.

Fields didn't get the time. He died from ulcers the year following his excursion. It wasn't until 1957 that his newspaper stories and diaries were published in book form under the title *Prairie & Mountain Sketches.*

Stewart's trip this time was relatively short; the party was back in St. Louis in October. It had gone as far as the Wind River mountains, in present western Wyoming, had a small dustup with the Osages, killed some buffalo and saw one member of the working crew die after he pulled a loaded rifle, muzzle first, from a wagon. The ensuing shot killed him. There was a grand party with a band of Snakes, with feasting, gambling, hunting, and racing, on foot and horseback.

And there was a dandy fight, between Joseph Smith, one of Sublette's top men, and L.D. Walker, a hired hand. "The whole cavalcade stopped to witness it," William Clark Kennerly later told his daughter, "while Charboneau ran excitedly about, keeping a ring around the combatants with his heavy whip and shouting for no one to interfere." It wasn't a very fair fight, Kennerly said, because Smith was much bigger but when he jumped on Walker's back, Walker pulled out his pistol, and firing over his shoulder, shot Smith in the thigh, "the wonder being that he did not kill him." Smith survived.

Despite all the fun, not all of the swells were happy. They'd chaffed under ex-army captain Stewart's discipline; they'd had to stand guard at night! There was a two-day delay on the trip home while one of the hunters' wives had a difficult birth.

Dr. Stedman Richard Tilghman of Baltimore, who was making the trip too, had to assist her. (He billed Stewart $14 for his services). The idea of camping for two days while an Indian had a baby upset them. Finally, a group including Jeff Clark and Kennerly broke away from the company and headed home, arriving several days ahead of Stewart.

One of the great parties of the West had ended. Stewart never returned to America.

Baptiste wasn't quite quit with Stewart. In the spring of 1844 he again headed west, this time with Solomon Sublette, William's brother, in hopes of capturing some animals to ship to Stewart in Scotland. He'd already had some young buffalo sent there. Solomon wrote to his brother A.W. Sublette from Fort William on the Missouri that he was leaving for the mountains with Baptiste to try to "Ketch Some big horns and Antelopes" but that "From inquiries it seems doubtful about getting sheep [the Bighorns]. T. Goodell who has been in that country for more than 3 years has gone to the other side of the mountain for the same reason."

It isn't known whether they succeeded.

By the summer of 1844 Baptiste was employed as a hunter at Bent's Fort, a key trading post for travelers headed either to the Rockies or to Santa Fe. Built about 1833 by the Bent brothers and their partner St. Vrain, it was some forty miles miles south of today's Pueblo, Colorado, on the Arkansas River. Chittenden, the historian of the fur trade, called it "the great cross roads station of the Southwest. The north and south route between the Platte River country and Santa Fe, and the east and west route up the Arkansas and into the mountains, found this their most natural trading point."

The fort was huge. Built of adobe, the walls were fourteen feet high and thirty inches thick and enclosed an area one hundred twenty-eight feet by one hundred thirty-seven feet. Inside were about twenty-five rooms, fifteen by twenty feet each, facing into the courtyard. On one side a second story of apartments was built. At two corners rose towers eighteen feet high, equipped with weapons.

It was indeed a fort.

Behind the fort was a corral about the size of the fort with walls six feet high.

Matt Field, the writer who travelled with Sir William Drummond Stewart, visited Bent's Fort in 1839 and wrote that it could accommodate two hundred men and four hundred animals.

The fort was to play an enormous role in the history of the settlement of the West, as traders and soldiers used it as a refitting spot on their advances to California and into the Spanish Southwest.

In July of 1844, Capt. John Charles Fremont pulled in with his company, led by Kit Carson, returning from his second expedition to the west. Many people in the east were anxiously waiting for his return, because he was bringing back what were expected to be definitive maps and there were thousands who wanted to set out for the Pacific Northwest—if they knew how to get there.

Just as important, there were two problems concerning possible expansion of the growing nation. There was the running dispute with Mexico over Texas and the southwest territories. And there was another, equally important: Just whose territory was that in the Northwest? The British maintained that the area south of what became British Columbia, the territory that eventually became the states of Oregon and Washington, was theirs while the U.S. claimed the region north of the Oregon country.

Fremont's maps were expected to help America's claims to the area.

William M. Boggs, a son of the governor of Missouri, had spent most of the winter of 1844 with William Bent in a place called Big Timbers, about eighty miles south of the fort, trading for buffalo robes; he lived in a tepee with a Cheyenne chief called Cinemo, later killed, while unarmed, by a panicky soldier. Boggs also spent time at Bent's Fort, and there ran into Baptiste Charbonneau. He learned a lot from the hunters there, he wrote, "particularly from Charbenau, an educated half breed. His father was a French Canadian, his mother said to be a Blackfoot Indian squaw." She wasn't, of course; she was a Snake, or Shoshone. Boggs added that "It was said that Charbenau was the best man on foot on the plains or in the Rocky Mountains."

Boggs then provided the only bit of physical description of Baptiste to be found although the sentence was a charming non sequitur: "He had been educated to some extent; he wore his hair long—that hung down to his shoulders." Many Indians and trappers did, of course.

In Hebard's book *Sacajawea,* there is a reproduction of a painting titled "Prince Paul, Baptiste, and the Indians." It purports to show Prince Paul, the German who took Baptiste to Europe, dressed in black and seated on the ground under an enormous leaning tree; there are six other equally large, unidentifable trees in the background. He appears to be conversing with the figure identified as Baptiste. Baptiste, also seated, on something, is naked to the waist and perhaps wearing only a breechcloth. His hair is in a top knot and hangs down to his back and he holds a long pipe. The two are surrounded by naked and half naked Indians and a few trappers. Based upon their proportions as painted, Baptiste is very tall and lean. The caption of the picture says "From an original painting by Mollhausen in Stuttgart, Germany; never before reproduced."

Dr. Hebard indicates the painting was found by a researcher she hired, in Stuttgart. An artist named Heinrich Baldwin Mollhausen did travel with Prince Paul in America—but not until the Prince's trip of 1849-1851. It is impossible that the Prince and the painter met Baptiste in these conditions on this trip, if ever, and the meeting of Paul and Baptiste in 1823 was under different circumstances. The painting as attributed is preposterous. So, unfortunately, it is no help in determining

Baptiste's appearance. (Mollhausen emigrated to the U.S. in 1849 when he was twenty four, and after his trip with Prince Paul signed on with an army boundary survey expedition, traveling across Arkansas, Texas, New Mexico and Arizona, reaching Los Angeles in 1854. Three years later he made still another surveying trip, up the Colorado River more than five hundred miles to the Grand Canyon, then back east via the Sante Fe Trail. He painted and sketched all the way. The Amon Carter Museum in Fort Worth has a collection of his watercolors of the Colorado. He may have met Baptiste on one of these trips, but not with Prince Paul).

However, in 1999 the German researcher, Monika Firla, found the painting in a museum in Bad Mergentheim. After studying the painting, two printed reproductions and a lithograph of the same scene with a caption, she concluded that the painting was made by Prince Paul himself and that it represented his meeting with two Kansa Indian chiefs on the Blue River near the mouth of the Kansas.

There is another, finer, painting of Baptiste, by the American artist John F. Clymer, in a private collection in Arizona. Titled "Down the South Platte, Baptiste Charbonneau," it shows him striding along a sand bar while two men wading in the shallow water drag a loaded canoe. Two other boats are in the background. The river is lined by trees. Baptiste appears to be about six feet tall, with broad shoulders and a narrow waist. He wears a broad-brimmed hat and carries a rifle casually slung over his shoulder. His shirt is brownish-red and his belt holds a tomahawk and pouches for power and balls. His pants are gray and on his feet are boots or moccasins with leggings nearly to his knees. He is a handsome figure.

Unfortunately, it is purely a work of imagination. Clymer wasn't born until 1907. After a long and successful career in the east as an illustrator—he created eighty covers for *The Saturday Evening Post* magazine—he "retired" in 1964 to return to his native west. Peggy and Harold Samuels, in their book *The Illustrated Biographical Encyclopedia of Artists of the American West,* say Clymer "achieved more fame in a few years with his historical paintings of the Northwest than in his whole career as an important illustrator."

But he was far too late to have seen Baptiste.

Boggs also wrote that there was another half-breed at the fort he called Tessou, who was "in some way related to Charbenau," although he didn't know how. Both Baptiste and Tessou "were very high strung," Boggs said, giving as an example that the latter fired a rifle from across the court of the fort at the head of the large negro blacksmith, "only missing the skull about a quarter of an inch," because the man had been in a group that chivaried Tessou the night before. Because St. Vrain decided Tessou was dangerous, he gave him an outfit and sent him away.

LeRoy R. Hafen, the historian who edited Boggs's manuscript, speculated that "Tessou's" real name might have been Toussaint and that he was Baptiste's half brother, though no parents were identified. Nothing more was heard of "Tessou."

Boggs also told of a horrific medical procedure undergone by William Bent while the two were at their camp below the fort in the winter of 1844. Bent had contracted a severe cold and sore throat, so bad that his throat closed and he couldn't swallow food. His Indian wife fed him by taking a mouthful of broth and squrting it through a quill which she forced down his throat. Writing on slate, he told Boggs he was going to die if he didn't get relief soon.

Bent sent for a Cheyenne Indian doctor known, oddly enough, as Lawyer. When the Indian arrived he examined Bent's throat by pressing the handle of a large spoon on his tongue, "just as any doctor would do." He then left and soon returned with a handful of small sand burrs. They were about the size of large peas with sharp barbs on them. "They were so sharp that by touching them they would stick to one's finger." The Indian then took a piece of sinew, made five or six threads of it, then pierced a hole through each burr and ran the threads through them to a knot at the end. He covered the burrs with marrow, took a small, flat stick, "about like a China chop stick," and with it forced the burrs down Bent's throat "the length of the stick." He pulled them out and repeated the treatment three or four times, in the course of which he pulled out "all the dry and corrupt matter each time." Bent's throat opened. He could swallow soup and in a day or two could eat food, and soon recovered.

Boggs commented that the Indian, whom Bent praised for saving his life, was laughing all the time he forced the burrs down the trader's throat. "No one but an Indian would ever have thought of resorting to such a remedy."

Medical care in the mountains wasn't for the fainthearted. In his autobiography, Kit Carson told of another medical procedure that was even worse. One of his party, Andrew Broadus, was pulling his rifle out of a wagon when it went off, the shot hitting him in the arm. "His arm began to mortify and we all were aware that amputation was necessary," Carson said. "One of the party stated that he could do it…The doctor [who may have been Carson; historians differ on his involvment] set to work and cut the flesh with a razor and sawed the bone with an old saw. The arteries being cut, to stop the bleeding, he heated a kingbolt from one of the wagons and burned the affected parts, and then applied a plaster of tar taken off the wheel of a wagon.

"The patient became perfectly well before our arrival in New Mexico."

The great Jim Bridger underwent one of those trail surgeries. He was carrying in his back an arrowhead picked up in a fight with the Blackfeet—Osborne Russell called these encounters "scrimmages"—three years earlier. Dr. Marcus Whitman, the missionary, showed up at the 1835 rendezvous and Bridger asked him to see whether he could get it out. Samuel Parker wrote that the arrowhead was iron about three inches long. "It was a difficult operation, because the arrow was hooked at the point by striking a large bone, and cartilaginous substance had grown around it. The Doctor pursued the operation with great self-possession and perseverance;

and his patient manifested equal firmness"—without the benefit of anesthetic, of course. The operation was a success and when Bridger was asked how he'd survived the wound for more than two years, he replied, "Meat don't spoil in the mountains."

Twelve years later Whitman was murdered by the Cayuse Indians at his mission near Walla Walla, Washington, along with his wife and twelve others, including the young daughters of Bridger and Joe Meek.

Baptiste was at Bent's Fort when Captain Fremont, whom he'd already met twice, showed up in 1845, with troops, outward bound on his third trip to the West. With him was Lt. James W. Abert, of the U.S. Corps of Topographical Engineers, who was going off to the southwest to explore and map Purgatory Creek and the waters of the Canadian and False Washita rivers. Colonel John J. Abert, the corps commander who also was Lt. Abert's father, had wanted Fremont to lead this exploration. But the Pathfinder had a mind of his own and a powerful father-in-law, Senator Thomas Hart Benton of Missouri. Fremont wanted to go to California again and knew Benton, who had been whooping it up for western expansion, supported him on that. So Fremont split off a detachment of 33 men headed by Abert and sent him off with the veteran mountain man Tom Fitzpatrick, who had been a guide for Fremont's second expedition to the West, in the lead as company guide. Fremont, as he wanted, headed to California.

Before he left Abert had an unexplained encounter with Baptiste Charbonneau. "On Saturday, the 9th," [of August, 1845], he reported, "Mr. Chabonard called for me to accompany him on a visit to 'Nah-co-men-si,' or the Winged Bear, more generally known as Old Bark. He is second in rank to 'Yellow Wolf...'" Yellow Wolf was the chief of a local band of Cheyennes and the previous day had sat for a sketch by Abert, an accomplished artist.

Yellow Wolf turned out to be an art critic. Abert related that "After finishing the sketch, I showed him my book, when, seeing some of his tribe whose likenesses were colored, he evinced great dissatisfaction, and said I had represented him badly...".

Abert's expedition wasn't totally successful, although he completed the journey without losing a man. A principle objective was to determine the origins of the Red River. Various disputed treaties said the river was a boundary for the new Republic of Texas, Mexico and the United States; the expedition was to establish, with precision, those boundaries. But Abert made a geographical mistake. He and his guides mistook the North Fork of the Red River for the Washita River, and thus failed to clear up the boundary question. In addition, the expedition was short of measuring instruments, having only one sextant and chronometer and not even a barometer. As the result, the editor of Abert's journal commented about the first calculation of latitude and longitude taken by Abert, "This is the only almost exactly correct observation made by the expedition."

Nevertheless, the expedition was the first in history to make the six hundred-mile trip from Bent's Fort to the settlements via the Canadian River with wagons, and without a fight with Indians.

Baptiste isn't listed on Abert's roster of the expedition. But Ann W. Hafen, the historian who wrote a brief profile of Baptiste for the series *The Mountain Men*, stated that "The Mountain Man, Thomas Fitzpatrick who was also with the party, expressed his delight at the usefulness of the guide, 'Mr. Chabonard.'"

7

WEST WITH THE MORMONS

Whether Baptiste was on the Abert expedition or not, there's no doubt about his next journey. He had a prominent role as guide, hunter, water- and camp-finder in the march of the Mormon Battalion to California.

The Mormon Battalion was another of those extraordinary events of the settlement of the West. The polygamous Mormons—formally the Church of Jesus Christ of Latter-day Saints—had been steadily moving westward from their founding in New York state, driven out of settlement after settlement by anti-Mormon mobs; twice they were burned out, shot out and threatened out of Missouri communites. It was in that state that Governor Lillburn W. Boggs, the father of the Boggs whom Baptiste had met at Bent's Fort, told the head of his militia, "The Mormons must be treated as enemies and must be exterminated or driven from the State if necessary for the public peace—their outrages are beyond description." The militia and others set to that goal with enthusiasm. Rioters had murdered the Mormon leader, the prophet Joseph Smith, and his brother in the Carthage, Illinois jail in 1844. Their most recent settlement was Nauvoo, Illinois, built on a point of land sticking out into the Mississippi River opposite Lee County, Iowa.

But time had run out for the Mormons there, too. After Smith's death, word was circulated of "wolf hunts," meaning invitations to those so inclined to burn Mormon homes, run off their stock and kill some Saints. The latter did some riding, raiding and shooting, in turn.

So under their new leader, Brigham Young, the Mormons began another exodus, across the Mississippi. Before long there were some twenty thousand of the Brethern strung out in a line four hundred miles long from the river to Council Bluffs, Iowa. They were living off of whatever they had been able to load into wagons.

It was with disbelief when U.S. army recruiters showed up to enlist five hundred Mormon volunteers into the army. It was the U.S. government, after all, that had failed to protect them from the mobs across the country.

What they didn't know at the time was that Brigham Young had sent a man to Washington, D.C., to ask President James Polk for help. Young offered to haul supplies for the army, build posts or provide any other service that would earn enough to buy wagons, teams and supplies to take his people west.

President Polk had been elected in 1844 on the promise that both the new Republic of Texas and the Oregon country would be taken into the union. In February, 1845, Congress voted in favor of annexation. A month later, the Mexican government, which already had lost Texas and certain that the U.S. wanted even more of its territory, broke off diplomatic relations with the U.S. Polk began preparing for war. In January, 1846, Polk ordered General Zachary Taylor to march to the Rio Grande River, claiming it as the western boundary of the country. The Mexican claimed the boundary was one hundred miles to the east and that Taylor's march was an act of war.

The war started in April when Mexican troops crossed the Rio Grande and attacked Taylor's troops. The U.S. declared war. Polk then ordered General Taylor to conquer Mexico City and another army to invade Chihuahua, Mexico from San Antonio. Colonel Stephen Watts Kearny was directed to conquer New Mexico and California, both territories still claimed by Mexico.

It was with that background that Polk, after refusing Brigham Young's various proposals, ordered that Mormons be enlisted to fight the Mexicans. Colonel Kearny, who was at Fort Leavenworth, Kansas, building up the new Army of the West, called for five hundred Mormon volunteers and when they were slow in coming forward, Brigham Young ordered them to volunteer.

Kearny got his five hundred, and more. Thirty-one wives and forty-four children, along with some grandfathers, went along. That was at Council Bluffs, and the contingent headed to Fort Leavenworth to be swore in as soldiers in the U.S. Army. Kearny, with guide Tom Fitzpatrick in the lead, headed for New Mexico with a detachment of regular army troops and the Mormons followed later.

The Mormon soldiers' clothing allowances, $42 per man, and their pay—some $70,000 in all—went not to them but to Brigham Young; this was the way he hit upon to finance the Saints' journey to what became Utah, the destination recently picked. (Fremont, in his memoirs, said Young settled upon Salt Lake after reading his description of the country in his report to Congress after his expedition in 1843). It also financed Young. He used some of the money to buy food and supplies, which were shipped on his own freight line, which he then sold to his members out of his store at Council Bluffs, another of the Mormons' temporary settlements. He also sold whiskey, as long as it lasted. In April Young then took a "Pioneer Band" of one hundred forty-three men, three women, two children, seventy-three wagons, two hundred eleven horses, mules, and oxen and headed west. On July 24 the

Mormons arrived at the valley of the Great Salt Lake, one thousand four hundred miles from Nauvoo, Illinois, their former home.

The ragtag Mormon Battalion, wearing what was left of their civilian clothes, arrived at Santa Fe, which had surrendered to Kearny without a shot, on October 9 after a two-month march—a two-month hike, really, since the soldiers didn't know how to march—two months of complaining about the army officer in command and convinced that the army doctor attached to the battalion, George Sanderson, was trying to kill them. He dosed everyone on sick call with calomel.

The next week the Mormon Battalion got a new commander. His orders were to take this group of malcontents to California and to build a wagon road in the process.

Lieutenant Colonel Philip St. George Cooke was a Virginian, a graduate of West Point at 18, a regular Army officer and as such a disciplinarian. Three years before taking over the Mormon Battalion while in command of a large party of Dragoons Cooke had disarmed a hundred "Texians," a sort-of free lance army authorized by the Republic of Texas to intercept, and probably rob, Mexican traders headed for Santa Fe. He sent them home.

With the Mormons, he had his work cut out. He took a look at his troops and rendered a verdict:

"Everything conspired to discourage the extraordinary undertaking of marching this battalion eleven hundred miles, for much the greater part through an unknown wilderness without road or trail, and with a wagon train.

"It was enlisted too much by families; some were old, some feeble and some too young; it was embarrassed by many women; it was undisciplined; it was much worn by traveling on foot and marching from Nauvoo, Illinois; their clothing was very scant;—there was no money to pay them,— or clothing to issue; their mules were utterly broken down; the quartermaster department was without funds and its credit bad; and mules were scarce."

Later he noted that "The battalion have never been drilled, and, though obedient, have little discipline; they exhibit great heedlessness and ignorance, and some obstinacy."

He weeded out the sick, the old and the women. Eighty-six men, under two officers, and most of the women and children, were sent to the small settlement of Pueblo, where an early party of Mormons had gone to set up winter quarters. Five women, wives of Mormon soldiers, were allowed to join the troops on the march to California, supposedly as laundresses.

On October 19, the battalion started for California with only sixty days of rations. It had full rations only of flour, sugar, coffee and salt, salt pork for thirty days and soap for twenty.

It was a huge operation: twenty-five government wagons; three mule wagons for each of the five companies, pulled by eight mules; six ox wagons for heavy equipment, four mule wagons for the battalion command; five company wagons, purchased by the troops to carry their personal loads, and twelve family wagons.

Cooke's route west was down the Rio Grande, then across Chihuahua, now southern New Mexico, crossing the mountains near the San Guadalupe Pass. Then straight to the San Pedro River and then turn west to Tucson and from there straight northwest to the Gila River. From there the battalion would follow Kearny's route.

Baptiste was with the battalion, hired as one of four guides and hunters. While there's no doubt of Baptiste's prowess as a hunter, as his exploits with the battalion clearly showed, it's unclear why he was expected to act as a guide, too. He probably had been as far as Santa Fe while working for Jim Bridger and then Bent & St Vrain, but there's nothing to suggest he'd been much beyond there.

Baptiste traveled with Colonel Kearney's main column from Bent's Fort as far as Albuquerque. Captain W.H. Emory of the Topograpical Engineers, who was on Kearny's staff, wrote that "I saw some objects on the hill to the west, which were first mistaken for large cedars, but dwindled by distance to a shrub. Charboneau (one of our guides) exclaimed, 'Indians. They are Apaches.' His more practical eye detected human figures in my shrubbery."

But near Albuquerque Baptiste was assigned by Kearny to travel with the Mormon Battalion, as one of its four guides, while the Dragoons went ahead.

One of the guides didn't last long. Two weeks after departing from Santa Fe, Cooke reported, "I met one of the guides, whom Leroux, their chief, sent back, ostensibly to settle upon smoke signals, but really, I suspect because he was of no use. The fellow weighs two hundred pounds, and has been drinking for a week or two; I ordered his discharge."

As the battalion moved west, the course got rough. At the end of October, Cooke recorded that "...a sand hill reaching the river bank was encountered; two hours, with teams doubled, and twenty men to a wagon, were required to reach its top,—only three or four hundred paces." On November 9, Cooke wrote that "In six days, resting one, the battalion could only make forty miles, in about the same number of hours' work...

"This slow progress was over very bad ground, without a road;—deep sand, steep hills and rocks, ten miles together, without river-bottom land; the men, nearly all of them, laboring in aid of the weak teams to move the wagons."

Cooke also noted that game—bears, deer, and beavers—were showing up. Old habits died hard for Baptiste. "..some of the last were trapped by Charboneaux, an active half-breed guide."

Cooke began lightening up. He'd just learned that the route to California was three hundred miles longer than originally believed, that is, closer to 1,450 miles than 1,100. There weren't nearly enough rations. He noted that one meal alone required one cow and twelve lambs. He'd just purchased eighty sheep from a herder the battalion had passed. He sent a Lieutenant Smith with $100 and "ordered him to give the same price as yesterday and to *take them*." Smith got them.

So Cooke sent back to Santa Fe "fifty-five of the sick and least efficient men" and gave them rations for twenty-six days "but of flour only ten ounces to the ration and of pork, eight." At that point the battalion had been out twenty-two days. Cooke figured he'd be relieved of eighteen hundred pounds of rations in this manner and the rations the fifty-five men left with the battalion would increase the supply for the remainder. He also ordered that the tent poles be left at the camping spot; the troops' muskets would be used instead. Some tents were left behind. More weight saved. He figured the wagons were lighter by twenty per cent and the rations increased eight days.

Cooke also kept trying to instill some order. Earlier, he had put one of his captains under arrest and made him spend a day marching behind his company for staying overnight in Santa Fe without permission. On the trail he called the captains together and told them they had to be more diligent in seeing that the mules were properly fed and grazed. The officers, he noted wrly, "make excellent promises." He demoted one first sergeant to the ranks for failing to form his company at reville, "and giving the excuse that it was not light enough to call his role." He ordered two soldiers tied to the back of a wagon and march behind it all day, for, according to a Mormon soldier, failing to get up and salute an officer on his rounds. More likely they were asleep on post.

His efforts at discipline didn't endear him to the troops, although they appreciated that he was as severe with officers as with enlisted men. On top of that, he also had "a rare combination of swear words," which upset his religious wards.

It was all frustrating for the colonel. "All the vexations and troubles of any other three days of my life have not equalled those of the last twenty-four hours... My attention is constantly on the stretch for the smallest things. I have to order, and then see that it is done," he complained at one point.

And, as might have been expected, the battalion didn't know where it was going. "I have no guide that knows anything about the country," Cooke observed.

Not many people did. That was the reason that Colonel Kearny had drafted Kit Carson to lead his advancing troops to California. Carson had just ridden the so-called Gila route from California en route to Washington with dispatches from Fremont in California. Kearny ordered him back as guide, and gave the dispatches to Fitzpatrick, who had been guiding the army but didn't know the Gila route, to deliver.

Cooke was dismayed by that. "Did the General stop to think what it was he demanded?" he wrote. "A man had just ridden eight hundred miles over a desert,— a wilderness,—where he could meet no human being save a few savages likely to seek his destruction; (he rode ninety miles without halting, over a jornada of sand!) he had arrived at the verge of society, and *near the residence of his family!* He is required to turn right back, and for another year of absence! That was no common sacrifice to duty."

Kearny had tried to persuade Carson to turn back, but when the scout argued that he had a solumn duty to Fremont to deliver the papers to Washington, Kearny *ordered* Carson to join his army and lead the march.

The Mormon Battalion moved on. Baptiste was trying to help. He frequently ranged far ahead of the battalion, searching for a route for the wagons and for water. Cooke reported that "Charbonneaux has returned, and reports the gap in front of us to be practicable, and that there is water six miles on; he went with the others about twelve miles beyond it, without finding other water."

Baptiste was right. The gap was crossed "without much difficulty" and the water was found where it was supposed to be.

A few days later, Baptiste, who years before had made his displeasure with mules vocally known, took a more dramatic step to deal with one. Cooke explained: "Since dark Charbonneaux has come in; his mule gave out, he says, and he stopped for it to rest and feed a half an hour; when going to saddle it, it kicked at him and ran off; he followed it a number of miles and finally shot it; partly I suppose from anger, and partly, as he says, to get his saddle and pistols, which he brought into camp."

The next day Baptiste redeemed himself. "Whilst the train was crawling up the pass," Cooke wrote, "I discovered Charboneaux near the summit in pursuit of bears. I saw three of them up among the rocks, while the bold hunter was gradually nearing them. Soon he fired, and in ten seconds again; then there was confusing action, one bear falling down, the others rushing about with loud fierce cries, amid which the hunter's too, could be distinguised; the mountains fairly echoed. I much feared he was lost, but soon, in his red shirt, he appeared on a rock; he had cried out, in Spanish, for more balls. The bear was rolled down and butchered before the wagons passed.

"It is a fact that both shots—and the ball of the second, passed from hunter's mouth into the muzzle of his gun with only its weight to send it home—made but one hole in the bear's skin, in the side, and one ball ranged forward, the other back." Baptiste had loaded his gun for the second shot without taking time to use a ramrod and fired so quickly and accurately the second shot penetrated the same hole as the first. These were grizzlies and not usually dispatched with two shots. The dead one was eaten at dinner that night.

Cooke's problems with the route continued. The guides said it was impossible to follow the Gila river route proper, or that taken by Kearny, who had left his wagons behind. So a route south through Sonoma, Mexico, was decided on. But that country, too, was almost unknown to the guides and they recommended a loop back to the southeast before turning west again. Cooke said no; "he would be damned if he would go round the world to reach California." The battalion turned right, that is, headed west again.

Water was a constant problem. At one point when water was found, "it was not enough for the men to drink; it was soon gone and the poor fellows were waiting for it to leak from the rocks, and dipping it with spoons!" Another time the mules traveled forty-seven miles without water.

Cooke had hoped to buy mules from the Apaches, but it was no sale. The Apaches had distrusted Americans ever since they'd been treacherously treated ten years before. An American named Johnson had come up from Sonora ostensibly to trade with the Indians. After friendly gestures, some one hundred Apaches men, plus women and children, gathered around. At that point a swivel gun that had been hidden between two bags of flour and was loaded to the muzzle with balls and chain was fired, killing and maiming many Indians. In a subsequent battle, seven more were killed. So the Apaches weren't much interested in helping out.

The route continued difficult. To lighten the wagons in the Guadalupe Mountains in New Mexico when a deep ravine was encountered, half the goods were taken out and loaded on nearly one hundred fifty mules, which were sent ahead six miles, unloaded, brought back and the process repeated with the other half. Then the wagons were lowered down the ravine, on a track the soldiers had roughly cleared by pick and shovel, two or four teams of mules pulling while fifteen men hung onto ropes tied to the rear axles to keep the wagons from crashing into the mules.

All but one wagon survived. The next day the interpreter, Doctor Foster, accidently found a pass down the ravine about three miles from the difficult descent. One of the Mormons said Cooke became angry and said—probably shouted—that the guides were "ignorant of this country." Another commented that "No other man but Cooke would have attempted to cross such a place with wagons."

Food was less a problem than water although there were hungry days. On the western reaches there were hundreds of wild cattle, particularly bulls. One was killed only after it was shot twenty times, many of the shots at close range. The bulls were ferocious, attacking the columns without warning, to the point Cooke ordered the soldiers to load their muskets for protection. One ran at a man, caught him in the thigh, and threw him clear over its back, then charged a mule team, got its head under the first and tore out the entrails of the second. Another ran against a soldier, who escaped with bruises, and still another charged a horse tied to a wagon, then hit the wagon so hard it lifted it out of the track. A bull got two shots in the heart and two in the lungs and kept coming. Cooke noted, to still the doubters, "I have seen the heart."

Enough were shot to provide several meals.

The battalion reached Tucson, now of Arizona, but then considered Mexican territory, at least by the Mexicans. It was a military outpost of some five hundred people, two hundred of them soldiers. There had been frequent reports that a Mexican army was marching to attack the battalion, although none appeared and there were constant rumors of opposition and revolts. So there was reason for Cooke to be concerned. A little later, there was an uprising in New Mexico, behind the battalion, even though that territory was supposed to have been pacified in August when Colonel Kearny raised the American flag in Santa Fe. Charles Bent of Bent's Fort, who had been appointed governor of New Mexico by Kearny, was murdered, along with five others, by Indians and Mexicans, at Taos and nine Americans were killed elsewhere in the territory in January, 1847. The revolt lasted until July with a number of pitched battles between American troops and Mexicans and Indians; in one, more than one hundred fifty rebels and seven American soldiers were killed.

So Cooke wasn't surprised when at Tucson it looked as though there would be a battle when the Mormon Battalion arrived. Some Mexican outriders made defiant statements and Cooke tried to prepare his men for a fight. But "The soldiers didn't drill to his liking and he swore at them profusely...Even after additional drilling he still wasn't satisfied with the results." Despite the poor results, the battalion marched into town but when the troops arrived they found the town had been evacuated, the soldiers and most of the civilians gone, along with their possessions. Mexican troops that had come in from outlying posts in support of the Tucson detachment also had left.

The Americans raised the flag and moved on. Water continued to be scarce. One night after another dry day, the column spotted a fire ahead, the agreed signal for a water hole. "The march was continued; it was cloudy and very dark; after advancing a mile or two with difficulty over very uneven and bushy ground, the fire was reached, and found to have been made by a stupid guide for his own comfort," Cooke wrote disgustedly. The battalion had marched twenty-six of the last thirty-six hours; Cooke had been in the saddle for thirty-two of the last fifty-two hours.

The battalion arrived at the Pima Indian villages on December 21, and soon after the Maricopa Indians, and found them friendly, attractive—and to their amazement—honest. Although the Indians wove cloth blankets they were nearly naked, a fact that bothered some of the Saints. One, William Coray, wrote "..the women looked very baudy indeed, with nothing but a breech cloth. Many of them were singularly formed. Their bubbies were nearly eighteen inches long and looked unnatural."

Even though the Indians made cloth, they were avid to trade food for the soldiers' clothes; unfortunately the latter were in short supply. The soldiers swapped buttons from their clothes and even their ragged shirts and got cakes, corn, beans, meal, squash, molasses and watermelons in return. But there was much grumbling when the colonel told the troops they'd have to carry their purchases or leave them, to spare the mules.

Cooke was so impressed by the Indians' industry and honesty that he "decided to add to their comfort and welfare by introducing sheep among them," leaving three ewes with young, "which was the best I could do."

There were some two thousand Indians in the battalion's camp, all enjoying themselves. "It reminds me of a crowded New Orleans market," Cooke commented.

The next day's march was fifteen miles, entirely through cultivated grounds.

Despite the recent windfall from the Indians, Christmas dinner wasn't much: Cold beans, pancakes and pumpkin sauce.

The colonel still was trying to lighten the loads his worn-out mules were hauling. He cached three hundred mule shoes and their nails. For six days the marches averaged only ten miles, "an unremitting struggle with the rude barrenness of a rainless wilderness," the men pushing and pulling the wagons to help the mules.

At the end of December Cooke sent Leroux, his head guide; Baptiste Charbonneau, Hall and two others ahead. They were to round up any mules and cattle they could get and bring them back to the battalion. One was to stay at Warner's ranchero, a large, rich refuge for wayfarers owned by an American, and arrange matters for the battalion's arrival. The others, including Leroux, Baptiste and Hall, were to attempt to reach San Diego, three hundred miles away, and find out what was going on.

Because the military situation in Californiia was a mess. General Kearny's orders were to take New Mexico and California. He'd taken New Mexico. But there were complications galore in California.

Mexico had opened the borders of its provinces to trade in 1821 and the California coast was increasingly visited by American and British merchants looking for business. They liked what they saw. Americans in particular began arriving to stay, by ship and by overland caravans. Some of them took Mexican citizenship but not very seriously. And the more Americans who arrived, the more they talked of breaking away from Mexico and setting up their own republic.

At the same time, President Polk was sending troops to California for the express purpose of annexing the state. That was the purpose of Kearny's expedition and that of the Mormon Battalion. Polk also had ordered the navy, carrying a regiment of troops, to occupy the California ports if war broke out with Mexico, and it did, under Commander Robert Stockton, who was named chief of naval and land operations. Stockton promptly occupied the ports, and declared victory. Word was sent east that the war in California was over.

It was a short victory. The Californians—that is, the Mexicans—revolted against American rule and drove the Americans out of Los Angeles, and San Diego as well.

Meanwhile, the impatient Americans had declared the Bear Flag Republic in northern California and Capt. Fremont, who had been marching to and fro in California and up into Oregon territory, rushed to Sonoma and put himself in charge. His battalion of men from his survey crew and American volunteers formed the California Battalion—Capt. Fremont in command, of course.

Stockton sent word to Fremont to come south and help clean out the rebels. And he sent one hundred eighty of his troops to rescue Kearny because of an urgent message for help delivered as the result of an astonishing crawl and barefoot walk.

Kearny had suffered a disaster.

The fight had been brief but costly. In early December, at a hamlet called San Pascual, Kearney ran into a group of "Californians," that is, Mexican troops, blocking the road to San Diego, forty miles away. They were armed with muskets and long lances and riding well-trained fresh horses. Kearny's troops had just made the crossing from Santa Fe that was as hard as the trailing Mormon Battalion's would turn out to be. His men were riding half-dead horses and mules, many only half broken. Some of the troops were on foot.

The fight lasted about five minutes. When it was over Kearny had suffered two lance wounds and eighteen Americans were dead, including three officers. And the Californians had captured one of the howitzers that had been dragged all the way from Santa Fe.

The Californians dispersed, the Americans patched up their wounded and the next day started west again. But the enemy troops were skulking about and Kearny needed help. That night Kit Carson, who had been guiding the Dragoons since Santa Fe, pulled off another of the daring exploits that earned him his reputation.

Carson, Lieutenant Edward Beale, and Beale's Indian servant, slipped out of the camp with a call for help. They crawled on their bellies most of the night, being nearly discovered by the patrolling Californians many times. When they finally got past the enemy's lines, they'd lost their shoes, which they'd tied around their necks when they'd started crawling; they walked barefoot through the cactus. Separating so as to increase their chances of getting through, all three reached San Diego the following night. Beale had to be carried in and his health was broken by the ordeal; it took him two years to fully recover. Carson was in bad shape for several days. There's no record of how the Indian fared but he had made it to San Diego before the others.

As a result of Carson's message, Stockton sent the troops to Kearny, and the combined forces, with the road now open, marched to San Diego and occupied it. Then they marched up to Los Angeles and after a couple of skirmishes with Californians, who were losing heart, entered Los Angeles unopposed. The war for California really was over.

Fremont and his troops showed up after the fighting.

Meanwhile, the Mormon Battalion had reached the Gila River and Cooke decided to make a pontoon boat to load with baggage and some of the food and float it down the river; the idea was that the battalion would march down the river, with the boat putting in each night to supply the troops. He had two wagons lashed together between two cottonwood logs and two thousand five hundred pounds of supplies were loaded on.

The experiment failed. The boat didn't show up for five days and when it did it was empty. The river was supposed to be three or four feet deep but in fact it was only three or four inches in places and the cargo had to be unloaded. When the boat finally arrived at camp there was great consternation; the supplies had been left along the river bank. Mules were sent back and finally returned with only four hundred pounds of flour.

Short rations continued.

The battalion reached the mouth of the Gila, at the Colorado, on January 8. It took all night to get the troops across. It was cold; ice was an inch thick on the river's edges. They now faced one hundred miles of desert. And, though freezing at night, the heat was blistering during the day.

Cooke had been told there were old wells on the route. The first one he reached after a fifteen-mile march was filled in with sand. The men began digging and struck damp sand and then water. But the sides of the hole caved in as rapidly as they dug. Someone remembered that Susan Davis, the wife of one of the Mormon company captains, had a washtub in her baggage in one of the following wagons which she'd brought all the way from Nauvoo, Illinois. When the wagon arrived,

"Lieutenant Oman reported to me, to my astonishment, that they were unwilling to give up that valuable article!—upon which our lives seemed to depend," Cooke recorded. He ordered that it be confiscated. The bottom was punctured and the tub was set in the hole, water seeping in through the bottom, its sides keeping out the sand.

But grazing for the mules was scant and the combination of little water and less feed was breaking them down. Cooke kept leaving them behind and abandoning wagons. They were down to only seven wagons; they'd started with twenty-five.

At the next water hole, called Alamo Mocha, just over the Mexican border, wells again were dug out. It took eight hours to water the mules. Two more wagons were left. At the next, Pozo Honda, the water was so scarce it was issued by the gill. But there were thirty-five fresh mules, sent back by General Kearny, along with some cattle. There was a catch; the mules were unbroken. It took more than three hours to catch and harness them.

The troops were in increasingly bad shape. Many were without shoes, trudging over rough ground. They wore rough moccasins and even wrapped their feet in cloth; when an ox was killed they peeled off the skin of the lower legs and wore them.

On January 16 the battalion started marching at two a.m. and in mid-day reached a small, clear stream; everybody, including the mules, got as much water as they wanted. "The men arrived here completely worn down," Cooke wrote. "They staggered as they marched, as they did yesterday…It is astonishing to consider what the wild young mules performed and endured; driven thirty miles to meet me, then next day, in its heat, to go through the terrible process of being broken to harness—two hours of the most violent struggles possible; then to draw wagons two marches, and thus without food, to march the third day without water." Sixteen of them died.

The water made a big difference. Cooke was amazed. "The men, who this morning were prostrate, worn out, hungry, heartless, have recovered their spirits to-night, and are singing and playing the fiddle."

Part of their high spirits may have been accounted by the news that Cooke had received from two Indians bringing a message from San Diego: Kearny's troops had captured that city and were heading to Los Angeles and thus it appeared likely that the Mormon Battalion, which, after all, had been enlisted to fight the Mexicans, might not have to fight after all.

The message was in response to the arrival of Leroux, Baptiste and Hall in San Diego on January 14, two weeks after they'd started their three-hundred-mile trek.

But there still were hard days ahead. Reaching a canyon, Cooke found the pass too narrow for his wagons; it had to be chopped wider, which was difficult since the road-building tools had been lost in the boat. The first effort wasn't enough. A wagon was taken apart and carried through, and the cutting went on. The next wagon had to be carried through, also. Finally the cut the widen enough and the last two wagons, loads aboard, squeezed through.

The next day Baptiste Charbonneau showed up, alone, just six days after he'd arrived in San Diego, meaning he'd covered fifty miles a day on his return trip. The U.S. commander at San Diego had kept Leroux and Hall there, saying the road was unsafe because of hostile Californians. Just why it was safe enough for Baptiste wasn't said. Baptiste told Cooke there weren't many supplies in San Diego and suggested the battalion head to Warner's ranch.

The battalion continued, with the troops marching in front of the wagons in case of hostilities, and reached the ranch January 21; they saw their first houses in California.

There was food! The ration was increased to four pounds of beef a day, and a few days later to five pounds although one Saint complained there was no salt and another that Warner, "unlike the hospitable Pimas, he hid his bread and drove his cattle into the mountains."

There also was a band of San Luis Rey Indians, who had recently killed eleven Californians but had thirty-eight of their own killed in an ambush.

Jonathan Warner, owner of the ranch, warned that there might be considerable numbers of Californian troops retreating from Los Angeles, so Cooke drilled his troops and kept them in front of the baggage on the rest of the march.

But unthreatened, the Mormon Battalion reached San Diego on January 29, 1847.

And the next day Cooke issued an order that began, "The Lieutenant-Colonel commanding congratulates the battalion on their safe arrival on the shore of the Pacific Ocean, and the conclusion of their march of over two thousand miles.

"History may be searched in vain for an equal march of infantry. Half of it has been through a wilderness where nothing but savages and wild beasts are found, or deserts where, for want of water, there is no living creature..."

It continued in this vein at length, adding "Thus, marching half naked and half fed, and living upon wild animals, we have discovered and made a road of great value to our country."

Indeed they had. The rough wagon track the battalion had chopped out of the wilderness later became one of the major overland roads to the west and the basic route of the Southern Pacific Railroad.

Not entirely due to the Gentile leadership, of course. Saint Robert Bliss commented, "We have endured one of the greatest journeys ever made by man, at least in America, and it is the faith and prayers of the Saints that have done it."

But Cooke's complimentary order did much to soften the Saints' hearts toward their commander. He had, after all, gotten them safely to California. Recorded Mormon John Riser: "Had it not been for the cool headedness and sagacity of our stern commander...we must all have perished before reaching our destination."

The Mormon soldiers still had six months to go on their army enlistments, and the final sentences of Cooke's order made that clear: "But much remains undone. Soon, you will turn your attention to the drill, to system and order, to forms also, which are all necessary to the soldier."

It sounded very much like boot camp, and was.

By order of General Kearny, the Mormon Battalion was marched some more, this time fifty-three miles north, to the mission at San Luis Rey, four miles east of present Oceanside, and occupied it. There hadn't been much food in San Diego and no supplies; many of the men hiked in their bare feet. One Saint noted that the Battalion now was one hundred three days from Santa Fe, which they'd left with sixty days of rations. And they'd lost several hundred pounds of flour on the Gila. But after a supply ship from the Hawaiian islands arrived in San Diego, food began to arrive in quantity; it no longer was much of a problem.

San Luis Rey mission was founded in 1798 and flourished. Within five years a large church, four granaries, and quarters for Indian men and women had been built. It was surrounded by farm fields and orchards.The buildings, built of adobe, were connected, and large: five hundred thirty feet feet by six hundred feet, forming a square, and within it orange trees were planted. By 1826 it had nearly twenty-nine hundred Indian converts—neophytes— and in 1832 it had more than fifty-seven thousand cattle, sheep, goats, pigs, horses and mules on its lands. But like the twenty other California missions, it was secularized in 1834 and went into decline. By 1844 there were only four hundred Indians living there. It was sold two years later to Jose Antonio Pico, for $2,400, and when the Mormon Battalion arrived in early 1847 it was in bad condition. Among other problems, it was infested with fleas in the dormatories, which the Saints never got rid of.

Cooke "immediately commenced a thorough practical instruction of the battalion in tactics; the absence of books made it a difficult and laborious task,— teaching and drilling officers half the day, and superintending, in the other half, their efforts to impart what they had just imperfectly learned. But all were in earnest, and in a very few weeks the complete battalion exercises were mastered."

It wasn't easy. One Saint said it was the first time he'd been taught how to turn around in formation. Discipline was tightened. Five men were put in stocks for walking through the Colonel's quarters and other offenses. Two men were reduced in rank for insubordination. Troops were ordered to cut their hair and shave off their beards, a disappointment to some who wanted to show off their growth to their wives when they finally reached them.

When they weren't learning the military life, the Saints worked cleaning and repairing the buildings, in the fields and in San Diego, where one company was sent to do the same thing. They still were badly clothed. Dr. John Griffin, assistant surgeon of Kearny's Dragoons, commented of the San Diego detachment, "They are bear footed and almost naked."

There was urgency in the drilling and the stiffening discipline because there still was the possibility that the Battalion would have to fight, although just who the enemy would be was in doubt. There were constant reports that the Californians were gathering troops to rebel against the Americans.

There also was the problem of Capt. Fremont. Commodore Stockton had named him governor of California, and he refused to give up this glorious title when Kearny arrived in San Diego bearing orders that made himself military and civil head of the state. For a time, there was the prospect of the Americans of the Mormon Battalion in battle with the collection of American trappers, Californians who had surrendered, freebooters and others who made up Fremont's California Battalion. That's why the Mormons had been sent north.

Eventually, the political games ended without battles. The rebel opposition melted away. Kearney ordered Fremont back to Washington City for refusing to obey his orders, where he was court martialed, and convicted on three counts. The court recommended leniency, so President Polk ordered Fremont back to duty. He resigned the Army, instead.

And went into politics, in which he'd been indulging all along.

Within a few months, President Polk achieved all his goals. The Mexican war ended with the signing of the Treaty of Guadalupe Hidalgo, in February, 1848. Mexico lost forty per cent of its territory and 530,000 square miles were added to the United States, including all of present-day New Mexico, Nevada, Utah, Arizona and California, and parts of Colorado, Idaho, and Wyoming. The Rio Grande became the boundary between the two countries. Polk paid a bargain $12 million for the lands north of the river.The 1846 settlement of the boundary dispute with England already had added what became Washington, Oregon and most of Idaho.

Manifest Destiny, the term first coined in 1845 by a New York editor to describe the widespread belief that it was God's will for Americans to occupy the continent, had prevailed.

Baptiste Charbonneau went to San Diego with the Mormon company sent there. On April 26, Lydia Hunter, wife of Mormon Captain Jesse Hunter, one of the four women who had accompanied the battalion the whole way, died, a week after giving birth to a boy. She had been pregnant the entire trip from Fort Leavenworth. A Mormon diarist commented that Baptiste was, in unspecified ways, "very kind and helpful to Captain Hunter during this sad time."

A small garrison was left at San Luis Rey and the rest of the Mormon companies marched to Los Angeles, then a town of about five thousand Mexicans and Indians. Town life caused problems for the Saints. Within a few days a mass meeting was held and the troops were harangued about the evils in the battalion—drunkenness, swearing and other unspecified sins. A vote, passed unanimously, called for the leadership to use its influence to stop these vices.

On July 4, there was a parade and "guns were shot twenty-eight times, once for every state in the union," and on July 16, the one-year enlistments of the Mormon Battalion ran out. A few men reenlisted. A few decided to stay in California. But most headed east, toward Utah, to find Brigham Young and their families.

The Mormon Battalion was no more.

In August, Colonel Richard Mason was appointed governor and commander in chief of U.S. forces in California by President Polk. Mason replaced General Kearny, who was heading for Washington, D.C., taking Colonel Cooke with him, and also Captain Fremont, who, when they reached Fort Leavenworth, was placed under arrest.

Mason then named Captain Hunter, late of the Mormon Battalion, who had reenlisted, Indian subagent in the southern part of the territory with headquarters at San Luis Rey. The order to Hunter told him to take an inventory of property belonging to the mission, the farms, horses, cattle and property. He was to consider himself the agent of the property, to guard it from abuse or destruction "and more especially to see that *no damage or descration is offered to the church or any other religous fixture.*"

He also was told to take "protective charge" of all the Indians living at the mission and in the neighborhood, "to draw them gradually to habits of order."

For all that he was to be paid $750 a year.

The order was signed W.T. Sherman, First Lieutenant, Third Artillery, Tenth Military Department Headquarters, Santa Barbara. That was William Tecumseh Sherman, who nearly twenty years later would win fame, or infamy, for his march through Georgia.

The next day Governor Mason sent an order to Hunter, telling him that if any Catholic priests showed up at the mission they were to have any quarters they wished, any produce from the farms they wanted, and "the entire management of the Indians, so far as it relates to their connection with the Mission..."

In November Mason sent a blank appointment for alcalde—in effect, magistrate or justice of the peace—for the mission to Colonel Jonathon Stevenson, who now was military commander for the southern district.

The appointment was to be filled out with the name of J.B. Charbonneau, or anybody else Stevenson wanted.

Stevenson named Charbonneau.

Why Baptiste? Probably because he was well known from his service with the Mormon Battalion. The fact that he'd helped Captain Hunter when his wife died probably helped. Or maybe because he was half Indian and he was going to be dealing with Indians. Maybe because he spoke Spanish as well as English and he was going to be dealing with Mexicans.

Some support for the latter is suggested by a copy of a lettter that Baptiste wrote in his position as alcalde. The letter appears in Irving W. Anderson's booklet, *A Charbonneau Family Portrait,* published by the Fort Clatsop Historical Association in 1982. The letter is in Spanish, dated May 9, 1848, and addressed to Jose Ant. Pico, the Mexican owner of the mission, and signed by Charbonneau. It says, "The Indians of Las Flores want you to do them the favor of sending some cowboys to gather up their cattle and to see if perhaps there are some at Las Pulgas."

In any case, Jean Baptiste Charbonneau, forty-two years old, half Indian and half French Canadian, was now an official of the government of the United States.

The job didn't last long. Baptiste resigned in July, 1848.

The circumstances of his resignation are murky. In a letter to Governor Mason, Colonel Stevenson "Encloses the resignation of J.B. Charboneau as Alcalde for San Luis Rey, and says that he has done his duty to the best of his ability but being 'a half-breed Indian of the U.S. is regarded by the people as favoring the Indians more than he should do, and hence there is much complaint against him.'"

However, it appears to have been more complicated than that.

The changes in authority in California and at San Luis Rey unsettled the Indians, and there are suggestions that Baptiste was somehow involved in a planned insurrection. Historian Ann Hafen found, in the Bandini Documents of the San Diego Archives at the Bancroft Library in Berkeley, a statement from Baptiste that strongly suggests that he was so accused and that there was some kind of investigation of that earlier in the year. The following is as printed in Hafen's sketch of Charbonneau published in 1976 in *The Mountain Men:*

"I, John B. Charbonneau of St. Louis, State of Missouri, came to California in the service of the U.S. as a guide for the Mormon Battalion, under command of Col. Cook, and after being in California nine months was appointed Alcalde for San Luis Rey, within the district of San Diego...[He denies giving the orders sworn to by the Indians as above, and says:] I am prepared to prove that the Indian Paulino is guilty of what he has sworn to my charge, and I will prove in the trial that he has taken a false oath.'"

Unfortunately, those documents no longer can be found in the Bancroft, so it isn't known what was excised. But a researcher found, in Mrs. Hafen's papers in the Lee Library at Brigham Young University at Provo, Utah, photo copies of another statement by Charbonneau that obviously is related to the investigation. It reads:

"April 6th, S.Luis Rey:

Your Judgeship—Sir:

I have as I told Don S. Aguello at parting from our visit near San Merced rancho, got the individuals who had the impudence to use my name, or even to hint it, to Capt. Tomas of San Isabel, the two letter-bearers, the writer, or Geronimo's clerk, and the letter, which I have the honor to enclose to you, you will peruse and judge how much I am implicated, or what part I (have) taken in it. I hear that Geronimo has got to the Potiers and is collecting all his principal men to come here to the Mission. I will certainly send Geronimo as prisoner. If it is necessary that I should go down, I am ready to appear, as I think with you to see the Indians safe."

In a letter the following day, Baptiste says he is sending the Indians and "I feel anxious to have them tried." And he complains that "from the information which I got this morning, that the trial of these Indians was one that materially concerned me, and I was a little surprised to learn that an investigation was in progress without my being notified of it."

It is unknown who the people named in the two statements are (except that Geronimo is certainly not the famed Apache warrior), but it seems clear that Baptiste strongly denied being involved in an insurrection or anything else.

In any case, Colonel Stevenson accepted his resignation and recommended that the expenses of his office be paid from the civil fund, since the alcaldes served without pay.

There's another possible explanation for Baptiste's resignation. In 1921, in the series *The Missions and Missionaries of California,* Father Zephyrin Engelhardt published the history of the San Luis Rey Mission and in the course of his research examined an account book for 1847. It records, on a day by day basis, over ninety pages of the accounts of people who did business at J.A. Pico's general store and dram shop at the mission; he's the man who bought the mission for $2,400 in 1846.

Father Engelhart singled out a particular account, that of one Flujencio, although he said there were similar accounts for many other Indians and Mexicans. Flujencio was an Indian laborer whose wages were $3 a month—12 1/2 cents a day. He noted that two Americans also showed up in the accounts, but they were paid $20 a month and received their wages in cash. The Indians got very little cash, if any.

Flujencio was buying aguardiente (brandy or whiskey) and wine regularly, almost daily, at prices of one to six reales. His account for the years 1846 and 1847 show that he ran up a tab of 109.87 and 1/2 reales. Pico took the unfortunate Flujencio before Alcalde Charbonneau. The decision was equally unfortunate. Charbonneau found that Flujencio had worked off 58.30 of the total bill "by services" but had a balance due 51.37 1/2.

"I, J.B. Charbonneau, do sentence Flujencio to work in the services of Don Jose Ant. Pico at the rate of twelve and a half Cents per Day, until he (Flujencio) has paid said debt."

At this Magistrate's office, St. Louis Rey

April 24th, 1848

J.B. CHARBONNEAU

Alcalde

Wrote Father Engelhardt: "We can now very well understand why Charbonneau wanted to resign the office of Justice of Peace. It was distasteful for a decent man to sentence helpless Indians to slavery in order that they might pay for the liquor received in excess of the 12 1/2 cents, their day's wages for labor. If the Indian had a family, what of the wife and the children?"

Father Engelhardt also concluded that Pico was cooking the books. "How Jose Antonio Pico figured in order to make Flujencio's debt amount to $109.87 1/2 is incomprehensible. There is nothing more in the book than the wretched liquor accounts of 1846 and 1847, which show an indebtedness of only $22.50."

Owning a liquor store obviously was a good business then, as it is now.

Because of the damage liquor did to Indians, also then as now, one of Colonel Mason's first acts as governor was to outlaw sales to Indians. But the Reverand Father notes sadly that "Despite Mason's proclamation, the Indians and Mexicans secured the liquor." Father Engelhardt said that in his entire missionary career he had never heard "that a whiskey Indian turned informer against a liquor dispenser." His book included a sketch, artist unidentified, of drunken Indians on the road from San Luis Rey to Oceanside.The sketch was made, the Father said, by the eyewitness, and it was drawn forty years "after the mission period."

8

THERE'S GOLD ON THE AMERICAN RIVER!

One day in August, 1848, a Captain Newell sailed up the Willamette River in Oregon, buying up all the spades he could find as he went along. He also bought wheat, and when his ship was fully loaded, he told the puzzled locals that he was headed for San Francisco. Gold had been discovered in California.

Within days two-thirds of the able-bodied men of the state—the population of white men, women and children was about ten thousand at the time—dropped whatever they'd been doing and headed for California, according to Terence O'Donnell in his history of Oregon published in the *Oregon Blue Book*. The *Oregon City Spectator* newspaper pleaded with Oregonians to stay on the farm—until the paper's printer departed for the gold fields and interrupted publication.

The Oregonians were late in getting the news.

The previous January James Marshall, building a sawmill for John Sutter, had noticed some yellow flakes in the gravel from a sluice. The mill was at a spot now named Coloma, on the south fork of the American River, about fifty miles northeast of Sutter's Fort (today the fort is surrounded by the city of Sacramento).

Marshall and Sutter tried to keep news of their find a secret until Sutter—known as the King of California—could secure title to the land surrounding the mill site; he already had a grant of 48,000 acres in two locations in the valley. But of course it leaked out, first in whispers and then literally in shouts. Mormon Sam Brannan, who had shepherded a boat load of his fellow Saints to San Francisco, visited the gold fields in May and returning to San Francisco strode up Montgomery Street, "holding aloft a bottle of dust in one hand, swinging his hat in the other and shouting 'Gold! Gold! Gold on the American River!'"

Sutter didn't get his title to the land. His earlier grant had been made by the Mexican government in California, helped along by Sutter's taking Mexican citizenship. But now the Americans were in charge and Governor Mason refused to give out any land titles until the questions about Indian claims were resolved. So Sutter and Marshall made a deal with the Indians: $200 a year in goods for joint possession.

The rest of the gold fields were open to all comers, and come they did, from all over California and from Oregon.

Baptiste Charbonneau was among them.

Not everyone at first was impressed with the discovery. K.C. Kemble, editor of the *California Star* of San Francisco, which had reported the strike in March, visited the gold fields in April and returned home to announce them a "sham!" About the time his paper hit the streets, a half-pound of gold dust was put up for sale. Lieutenant Edward F. Beale of the U.S. Navy, the man who had crawled through the Californians' lines with Kit Carson, even though still ailing from his adventure was sent by Governor Mason to Washington, D.C. with news of the find. Beale sailed to Mazatlan, crossed Mexico and then sailed north, arriving in Washington in early June. He interrupted President Polk at a chess game. In his *History of Placer County, California,* published in 1882, Myron Angel reports that "The story of the gold was received with a smile of incredulity, and the messenger was bantered by the august officials with the remark that the officers were probably speculating in city lots and wanted to induce an immigration; or were unduly excited over an unimportant discovery, and he was sent back with dispatches to Governor Mason."

But Mason went to the gold fields himself and wrote an official report, announcing the discovery as real, and big, as did Lieutenant William T. Sherman.

To add weight to his dispatch, Mason gave Lieutenant Beale a lump of gold as big as a potato, and sent him back to Washington, where he arrived in September.

This time President Polk was a believer, and in a few days announced the discovery to Congress. Beale went on to New York and with a friend visited Wall Street and from the steps of the Stock Exchange showed the lump of gold to a crowd that grew by the minute until the street was blocked.

At least, that's Angel's version. H.H. Bancroft, in his massive series on western history, says that the second trip to Washington City was made by a Lieutenant L. Loessen of the Third Artillery, who carried either "a tea caddy with 230 ounces, 15 dwts [pennyweight], 9 gr [grains] of gold," or "a small chest called a caddy with $3,000 worth of gold in lumps and scales," which had been purchased by a government agent for $10 an ounce. No mention of a potato-sized lump of gold nor of a trip to Wall Street.

In either event, Polk did announce the find to Congress on December 5, gold fever hit the country and the Forty-Niners were on their way.

Thomas Buckner was one of the Oregonians who was in the gold fields early. He was in a company of sixty-two from the territory who arrived at Sutter's Fort in August of 1848. A party of sailors arrived from the mines with "a considerable quantity of gold-dust," according to Angel's history, and told a friend, J.D. Hoppe, where they found it and allowed there was more where that came from. Hoppe promptly organized a party of seven, including Buckner, and set out for the "Sailor's Diggings." After a fall of uneven success digging in a canyon of the Middle Fork of the American River—using butcher knives, spoons, steel bars and pans—Buckner retreated to the Oakland area for the winter, working in a lumber mill. In the spring of 1849, he with two others returned to the diggings. According to Angel, they reached a gravel bar on the Middle Fork, where one, a Captain Merritt, who stuttered when excited, called out, "B-b-by G-g-god, he-he-r's wh-white man's ha-ha-r! Ye-yes, a-and Injun's ha-har, too."

Indeed there was. No bodies were found, but ashes of a fire near by indictated cremated bones of two or three people.

Buckner named the place "Murderer's Bar."

The trio decided the bar wasn't safe, however, and moved to another nearby, which was called "Buckner's Bar." The mining there was good but it wasn't long before Merritt decided to go down to visit the settlements and left in late May, promising to return soon. He didn't. The third, an Indian boy, decided to go find Merritt, and Buckner was left alone. Merritt, in fact, died a few weeks after leaving the mine, probably from over exposure to alcohol.

Angel recorded what happened next: "Toward the latter part of June, however, Tom Buckner's heart was gladdened by the appearance of other men, not hostile, at his camp, in the person of J.B. Charbonneau, Jim Beckwourth and Sam Myers, all noted mountaineers; and from that time onward came large crowds of gold-seekers, so that before the end of July, the river banks fairly swarmed with humanity above and below him for many miles."

Baptiste had found his home, there and nearby, for the next seventeen years.

Beckwourth was the guide, trapper and trader who spent time with Baptiste on the island in the Platte in 1842. He had a somewhat different version of how he and Baptiste got together. But Beckwourth's facts tend to be fluid and his accomplishments exaggerated, even though he did lead an adventurous life. In his autobiography, *The Life and Adventures of James P. Beckwourth,* Beckwourth said that "Becoming tired of my business in Sonora, for inactivity fatigued me to death, I disposed of my interest in it for six thousand dollars, and went on to Sacramento City with the money in my pocket. From this place I traveled on to Murderer's Bar, which lies on the middle fork of the American River; hence I found my old friend Chapineau house-keeping, and staid with him until the rainy season set in."

Murderer's Bar was not far from John Sutter's Hock farm, the place Prince Paul, Baptiste's European traveling companion, visited in 1850 and saw the Indian youth who reminded him so much of Baptiste. The Prince got the royal treatment from Sutter and was impressed with his organization.

"The Hock-Farm is one of the first to have been brought under cultivation in northern California," the Prince wrote. "Inasmuch as Mr. Sutter knew well how to win the friendship of the neighboring Hock Indians through humane treatment and generous hospitality, he was never in want for laborers."

However, when an old mountain man, the tireless tourist James Clyman, visited Sutter's Fort he had a different opinion.

"The Capt keeps from 600 to 800 Indians in a complete state of Slavery and as I had the mortification of seeing them dine I may give ashort discription," he wrote in his notebook. "10 or 15 Troughs, 3 or 4 feet long, war brought out of the cook room and seated in the Broiling sun all the Lobourers grate and small ran to the troughs like somany pigs and feed themselves with their hands as long as the troughs contain even a moisture."

127

Clyman played an interesting role in the West. He went to the mountains with the second trapping expedition of William Ashley and Andrew Henry in 1823, helping to recruit the company in "grog Shops and other sinks of degredation," commenting in his diary that the men who followed Falstaff were "genteel in comparison." He was thirty-one, much older than usual run of men making their first forays in the fur trade. Tom Fitzpatrick was twenty-four, Jedediah Smith a year older and Jim Bridger was nineteen. But Clyman, who was raised on a Virginia farm that belonged to President George Washington, had been hunting since he was fourteen, and after his family moved to Ohio, fought the Indians who were raiding the farms of the settlers and briefly was in the army during the War of 1812. He also worked as a surveyor and his eye for that work was reflected in the detailed diaries he kept as he traveled the west.

He is notable in western anals for four things: After becoming separated from his trapping companions, he walked, alone, six hundred miles in eighty days, from the Green River to Fort Atkinson at Council Bluffs. In 1823 he was with Jedediah Smith on a fur-trapping near the Black Hills when Smith was attacked by a grizzly. The bear broke his ribs and tore away his scalp at the hairline, exposing the bone of his skull and leaving his ear hanging loose. Clyman sewed the scalp and ear back and later recorded that "The bear had taken nearly all his head in his capacious mouth close to his left eye on one side and close to his right ear on the other and laid the skull bare to near the crown of his head...One of the captains ears was torn from his head out to the outer rim...Then I put my needle stiching it through and through over and over, laying the lacerated parts together as nice as I could with my hands." Smith recovered, and thereafter wore his hair long to cover his damaged ear. In the Black Hawk Indian War of 1832 Clyman served in a company of mounted volunteers; in the same company was Abraham Lincoln. Or, as Clyman put it, "Abe Lincoln served in the same company with me." And in

1846, heading east after having crossed the Sierras, he ran into an old acquantance from the volunteers, James Reed, who was leading an immigrant party west. "I told him to take the regular wagon track and never leave it—it is barely possible to get through if you follow it—and it may be impossible if you don't."

But Reed said there was a shorter route and "it is of no use to take so much of a roundabout course." Clyman renewed his warnings of the desert ahead and the rugged Sierras, and "that a straight route might turn out to be impracticable." But Reed ignored the advice.

It was the Donner Party.

James Beckwourth, who varied his trapping, trading, guiding and horse stealing with bouts of hotel, store and bar keeping, had been running a store in the Sonora mining country when he sold out and showed up at Murderer's Bar. It isn't clear by the accounts whether Baptiste had arrived earlier or whether, as Angel's history suggests, they arrived together; another account says Baptiste arrived first. But apparently they worked with Buckner as miners for a few months.

The miners—by 1850 there were fifteen hundred men working the diggings in the area— devised a scheme when the river ran low to dig a canal from the head of Buckner's Bar to a point below the end of Murderer's Bar. One of the rules governing the group stated that "any shareholder getting drunk during the time he should be on duty, shall pay into a common treasury of the company a fine of one ounce of gold-dust, and also forfeit all dividends during such time." The rule didn't stand up long. Once a week a pack load of whisky was brought in by an enterprising businessman and when he reached the top of hill leading into the canyon sounded a horn. His partner on the bar then fired off his gun, which announced that business was open. So many miners overindulged and thus were fined that the scheme soon collapsed and the ground was parcelled out into small claims to the members of the group.

Although the Murderer's Bar area was rich in gold, Baptiste obviously didn't hit it big, if at all. Because some time in 1849, James Haley White, who in his brief memoir said that he had gone to school in St. Louis with Baptiste, reported that "The last time that I saw this person [Baptiste] was in the year 1849 in passing on a road from Sacramento to Cold Springs to Placeville Cal. I stopped at a house for the night and it was kept by Jim Beckweth and John Baptiste Chaboneau."

White's reference to a house may have meant the kind of structure that was springing up along the American as the miners poured in. They were large tents, with canvas over frames and, usually, wooden floors. Beckwourth had opened his store in Sonora in such a structure, later replacing it with a frame building.

In any case, Beckwourth didn't stay around many months before going on to other pursuits but Baptiste was in the hotel-keeping business for a long time. (Another prospector who didn't stay around long was William Clark Kennerly, William Clark's nephew, with whom Baptiste had last crossed paths in 1843 when Kennerly made the excursion west with Sir William Drummond Stewart. Kennerly says he "dug diligently," but unsuccessfully, for several months before he "gave up in disgust" and went back to St. Louis. But he did come away with one of those stories that were heard all over the diggings. A short time after he gave up "a man who took my claim found a valuable vein right under our cabin, a few feet under the bed upon which I had been sleeping").

Beckwourth—whose name originally was Beckwith; he settled on Beckwourth for his book—was a great spinner of yarns, and his book records a dandy about Baptiste. By 1852 Beckwourth had a hotel and store in a valley near present Portola, the first business in the valley (the town now is named after him). It wasn't far from the Truckee, a river that reminded him of the St. Mary's River.

"The St. Mary's River is known to most persons as the River Humboldt, since that is the name that has been since conferred upon it, in honor of the distinguished

130

European traveler. I prefer the former name, as being more poetical, though less assuming. An Indian woman, the wife of a Canadian named Chapineau, who acted as interpreter and guide to Lewis and Clark during their explorations of the Rocky Mountains, was suddenly seized with the pains of labor, and gave birth to a son on the banks of this mysterious river.The Red-headed Chief (Clarke) adopted the child thus rudely issued into the world, on his return to St. Louis took the infant with him, and baptized it John Baptiste Clarke Chapineau. After a careful culture of his mind, the boy was sent to Europe to complete his education. But the Indian was ineffaceable in him. The Indian lodge and his native mountain fastnesses possessed greater charms than the luxuries of civilized life. He returned to the desert and passed his days with his tribe. Mary, mother of the child, was a Crow, very pleasing and intelligent, and may have been, for aught I know, connected with some of my many relatives in that tribe. It was in honor of this event and to perpetuate her memory, that the river received its original name, St. Mary's, and, as such, is still known to the mountaineers."

Beckwourth dictated his memoirs to T.D. Bonner and they were first published in 1856, long after the events described above. Some of the information Beckwourth must have picked up from Baptiste himself when they worked together. But the bulk is almost entirely wrong. Baptiste wasn't born on the St. Mary's River during the Lewis and Clark Expedition, but in the Mandan Indian villages before the expedition began its Western trek. Clark didn't take Baptiste with him to St. Louis; the boy was taken there by his parents several years later. The boy's mother most certainly wasn't named Mary, or called Mary, and she wasn't a Crow, she was Shoshone. And the expedition didn't go anywhere near the Humboldt, or St. Mary's, river, which is far to the south of its actual course.

But it is a swell story.

Baptiste stayed in the gold country for seventeen years. The historian Ann Hafen found, in the 1860 U.S. Census of Placer County, California, that the Secret Ravine post office, near present Auburn, listed John B. Charbonneau—[John being the Anglicized form of the French Jean]—male, aged 57, born in Missouri, and the *Directory of Placer County, 1861,* listing John B. Charbonneau as a clerk at the Orleans Hotel in Auburn, in the gold fields.

He did some other odds and ends besides hotel keeping. Placer County's semi-annual Treasurer's Report, dated December 2, 1852, shows payment to "John Charbonneau, services as Assistant Surveyor, $48," for the last six months of that year. He doesn't show up on any other accounts.

9

A DEATH IN OREGON

In the spring of 1866, Baptiste headed north, for the newly discovered gold fields in Montana Territory, back to the country in which he'd spent so much time years earlier.

In another of those odd coincidences that seemed to flourish in Baptiste's life, about the same time he was heading for the Montana fields, eleven hundred miles to the east his old trapping captain, Jim Bridger, was at Fort Phil Kearny, in Dakota Territory, helping map a road and negotiating with the Indians to give emigrants a full right-of-way to the gold fields of Virginia City, Montana. Philip St. George Cooke, Baptiste's old commander of the Mormon Battalion, now a general, as a cost-cutting move ordered Bridger fired as guide. The order was overruled and not long after William Tecumseh Sherman, now also a general, fired Cooke. To top the string of coincidences, old Jim Beckwourth, Baptiste's friend and former partner in the hotel business in California, was with Bridger. Beckwourth was sent to parley with the Crows, with whom he had lived and where he had been, maybe, a chief. But he died at the Indian camp before he could arrange a truce; he was sixty-eight, an old age for a hard-living mountain man. One legend says he was poisoned by the Crows; they wanted him to stay and lead them once again and when he refused they killed him. But more likely he just died from the hard effects of his rugged life.

Baptiste set out for Montana with two others, of unknown identity. He traveled from California into southeastern Oregon and in May crossed the Owyhee River at a ford just below where Jordan Creek runs into the Owyhee. He got wet, probably from swimming his horse across the river, which was high because of snow melt, and caught pneumonia. His unknown companions took him to Inskip Station, a stage stop about twenty miles east of the river, where he died on May 16. He was sixty-one. He had no known survivors.

On June 2, 1866, The *Owyhee Avalanche,* of Ruby City, Idaho, (absorbed by Silver City in 1867, which today has a year-round population of 10), published the following:

> *Died.*—We have received a note (don't know who from) dated May 16, '66, requesting the publication of the following: "At Inskip's Ranche, Cow Creek, In Jordan Valley, J.B. Charbonneau aged sixty-three years—of pneumonia. Was born at St. Louis, Mo.; one of the oldest trappers and pioneers; he piloted the Mormon Brigade through from Lower Mexico in '46; came to California in '49, and has resided since that time mostly in Placer County; was en route to Montana."

And in the July 7, 1866 issue of *The Placer Herald,* published in Auburn, the following notice appeared:

DEATH OF A CALIFORNIA PIONEER.—We are informed by Mr. Dana Perkins, that he has received a letter announcing the death of J.B. Charbonneau, who left this country some weeks ago, with two companions, for Montana Territory. The letter is from one of the party, who says Mr. C. was taken sick with mountain fever, on the Owyhee, and died after a short illness.

Mr. Charbonneau was known to most of the pioneer citizens of this region of country, being himself one of the first adventurers (into the territory now known as Placer county) upon discovery of gold; where til his recent departure for the new gold field, Montana, which strangely enough, was the land of his birth, whither he was returning in the evening of life, to spend the few remaining days that he felt was in store for him.

Mr. Charbonneau was born in the western wilds, and grew up a hunter, trapper, and pioneer, among that class of men of which Bridger, Beckwourth, and other noted trampers of the woods were the representatives. He was born in the country of the Crow Indians—his father being a Canadian Frenchman, and his mother a half breed of the Crow tribe. He had, however, better opportunities than most of the rough spirits, who followed the calling of trapper, as when a young man he went to Europe and spent several years, where he learned to speak, as well as write several languages. At the breaking out of the Mexican war he was on the frontiers, and upon the organization of the Mormon battalion he was engaged as a guide and came with them to California.

Subsequently upon discovery of gold, he, in company with Jim Beckwourth, came upon the North Fork of the American river, and for a time it is said were mining partners.

Our acquaintance with Charbonneau dates back to '52, when we found him a resident of this country, where he has continued to reside almost continuously since—having given up frontier

135

life. The reported discoveries of gold in Montana, and the rapid peopleing of the Territory, excited the imagination of the old trapper, and he determined to return to the scenes of his youth.

—Though strong of purpose, the weight of years was too much for the hardships of the trip undertaken, and he now sleeps alone by the bright waters of the Owyhee.

Our information is very meager of the history of the deceased—a fact we much regret, as he was of a class that for years lived among stirring and eventful scenes.

The old man, on departing for Montana, gave us a call, and said he was going to leave California, probably for good, as he was about returning to familiar scenes. We felt then as if we met him for the last time.

Mr. Charbonneau was of pleasant manners, intelligent, well read in the topics of the day, and was generally esteemed in the community in which he lived, as a good meaning and inoffensive man.

Both obituaries are replete with errors, of course. Baptiste was sixty-one, not sixty-three, when he died and he wasn't born in Montana, or St. Louis but in what was then Missouri Territory and now is North Dakota. And his mother wasn't a Crow but a Shoshone.

But the unnamed author of the latter article, even given the usual gentle treatment newspapers accord to the character of the recently departed, probably was accurate in *this* representation. Based upon what others said about him over the years, he *was* of pleasant manner, intelligent, well read, and a good meaning and inoffensive man. He also was well traveled, educated, excitable, tough and as a trapper, hunter and guide, "the best man on foot on the plains or in the Rocky Mountains." His old commander of the Mormon Battalion, Phillip St. George Cooke, was quoted (in an Associated Press story in 1966, original source unknown, unfortunately) as saying Baptiste was "humanity in confusion...near gentleman, near animal but above all capable, loyal and a most valued asset."

And he was the only member of the Lewis and Clark Expedition to return to Oregon, if only to die.

Not a bad life for a half Indian boy born of illiterate parents in an untamed country.

To the chagrin of historians, Baptiste left no diaries of his life, no journals, no memoir, and only the three letters, written while he was alcalde of Mission San Luis Rey, have been found. So the great question goes unanswered: Why did an educated man—far better educated than most of those with whom as an adult he lived, worked and fought—who had traveled widely in Europe and had been exposed to its culture at the highest levels, willingly spend so many years in the wilderness as a hunter, trapper and guide?

T.J. Farnham, meeting an educated Indian at Fort El Pueblo, not far from Bent's Fort, in 1839, asked him that question. The answer, as recorded in Thwaites' *Early Western Travels,* went on at length.

"For reasons found in the nature of my race," the Indian was supposed to have replied. "The Indian's eye cannot be satisfied with the *description* of things, how beautiful soever may be the style, or the harmonies of verse in which it is conveyed. For neither the periods of burning eloquence, nor the mighty and beautiful creations of the imagination, can unbosom the treasures and realities as they live in their own native magnificence on the eternal mountains, and in the secret untrodden vale."

The Indian went on to lament the bad effects that agriculture had on a wild country—moral and physical wretchedness among them—and the uselessness of science, since the Indian has his own senses upon which to rely. He ends in rejecting all that: "No. I must range the hills, I must always be able to out-travel my horses, I must always be able to strip my own wardrobe from the backs of the deer and buffalo, and to feed upon their rich loins; I must always be able to punish my enemies with my own hand, or I am no longer an Indian. And if I am anything else, I am a mere imitation of an ape...I shall live and die in the wilderness."

Whew. The speech obviously was polished to a high sheen by Farnham. Historian Ann Hafen says "this trapper prodigy may not be Baptiste Charbonneau." It definitely wasn't. Farnham himself said he was a Delaware Indian who went to Dartmouth.

But stripped of its flamboyance, the speech probably is close to Baptiste's sentiments. The wilderness *was* where his heart was.

The novelist Larry McMurtry, in his book *The Wandering Hill,* published in 2003, came to much the same conclusion. Speaking of Baptiste, McMurtry wrote: "Which was better: freedom with its risks, or the settled life with its comforts? It was not a question he could fully answer, but he did know that he himself belonged to the wild. He did not intend to go back to Europe. When he returned from Stuttgart, when he stepped off the boat at Westport Landing and looked again at the great Western prairies, it seemed to him that those prairies had been there all along in his head, even when he hunted in the forests of Europe."

Baptiste was buried just north of Inskip Station, in what became a small cemetery, containing his remains and those of two soldiers and two children. The land originally was private property, but the owner of the ranch donated it to Malheur County. The gravesite was rescued from oblivion by a Jordan Valley rancher, S.K. Skinner, in the 1960s and on August 16, 1971, the site was dedicated after the grave site was restored and a handsome marker was erected.

The marker read:

OREGON HISTORY

Jean Baptiste Charbonneau

1805 - 1866

This site marks the final resting place of the youngest member of the Lewis and Clark expedition. Born to Sacajawea and Toussaint Charbonneau at Fort Mandan (North Dakota) on February 11, 1805, Baptiste and his mother symbolized the peaceful nature of the "Corps of Discovery." Educated by Captain William Clark at St. Louis, Baptiste at age 18, traveled to Europe where he spent six years, becoming fluent in English, German, French and Spanish. Returning to America in 1829, he ranged the Far West for nearly four decades, as mountain man, guide, interpreter, magistrate and Forty-Niner. In 1866, he left the California gold fields for a new strike in Montana, contracted pneumonia enroute, reached "Inskip's Ranche," here, and died on May 16, 1866.

Among those attending the dedication were William Clark Adreon, great-great-grandson of William Clark, and historian Irving W. Anderson, the author of the sketches of the Charbonneau family. On March 14, 1973, the grave site was designated a Registered National Historic Place.

But it was neglected. In 2000, under the auspices of the Oregon Chapter of the Lewis and Clark Trail Heritage Foundation, the grave site was cleared of sagebrush, trees were planted and new posts installed around it. On June 24, 2000, it was rededicated. A flag with fifteen stars and fifteen stripes, similar to the one carried by the Corps of Discovery, was raised.

The gravesite is three miles off U.S. Highway 95 in the small community of Danner, seventeen miles west of Jordan Valley, in the southeastern corner of Oregon.

In 2000, the U.S. Mint issued a one dollar gold-colored coin bearing on its face the likeness of a young Indian woman, representing Sacagawea.

On her back is the papoose, Jean Baptiste Charbonneau.

The infant is shown peering over his mother's shoulder. That caused problems for the Mint because some sticklers for accuracy said that Shoshone women carried their babies on cradleboards and that the babies faced to the rear. In a statement couched in the solemn tones big government assumes on matters of importance, the Mint said, "The issue of how Sacagawea would have carried her baby is one that we at the Mint have spent a great deal of time examining. We have consulted numerous historians and Native American representatives on this topic, and we are comfortable with the historical accuracy of sculptor Glenna Goodacre's depiction."

It goes on: "Although the artist depicted Jean Baptiste facing forward on his mother's shoulder based partly on artistic considerations (the palette for the new coin is very small, and it was not artistically practical to depict the child facing backwards on a cradleboard) the artist believes and we agree, that as a matter of convenience, there were times that Sacagawea would have wrapped her baby up and carried him on her back."

There's strong historical support for this conclusion, the Mint said, having really dug into the subject. "According to Irving Anderson of the Lewis and Clark Trail Heritage Foundation, the Lewis and Clark journals are very vague in documenting how Sacagawea attended to Jean Baptiste. How Sacagawea transported her son is mentioned in Lewis's June 29, 1805, entry where he refers to 'the bier in which the woman carries her child.' Although no physical description of the 'bier' is provided, there is a reference elsewhere to mosquito netting as a 'bier.' Further, Sacagawea lived among the Hidatsa beginning around the age of 11, and although it is not conclusive that Sacagawea adopted Hidatsa customs, she could reasonably

A DEATH IN OREGON

have learned to carry Jean Baptiste slung from her shoulder as was the Hidatsa custom.

"Finally, we have spoken with Shoshone representatives who have relayed folk legend of how Sacagawea may have lost her cradleboard along the journey with Lewis and Clark. In any case, historians and other consultants have concluded that it is reasonable to assume that at some point on her journey, Sacagawea carried her son as Goodacre has depicted."

And with that the Mint rested its case.

The model for Sacagawea on the coin was, appropriately, a Shoshone woman named Randy L. He-Dow Teton. Interestingly, there was no model for Jean Baptiste.

By 2001, the Mint had poured out one billion of the Sacagawea dollars. But there were hardly any in circulation; people were holding on to them as curios or collector's items, apparently. So the Mint pumped out two hundred million more. Still they didn't circulate; at the end of 2001 the Mint found it had three hundred and twenty-four million in storage. So early in 2002 it stopped almost all production of the coin.

Today there are more statues of Sacagawea and other memorials than of any other woman in American history, from Washington, D.C. to Portland, Oregon. The most recent statue erected was placed in Statuary Hall in the rotunda of the U.S. Capitol, put there in October of 2003. It is a replica of one erected in 1910 on the grounds of the North Dakota capitol, in Bismarck. (And her name, as it is on the Bismarck statue, is spelled Sakakawea). She even has a crater on Venus—the Roman goddess of love—named after her. On maps of Venus her named is spelled with a "j" rather than a "g" on decree of the International Astronomical Union.

141

POMP

On every statue, peering over her shoulder or looking out at the world from her back, is her boy, Jean Baptiste Charbonneau, just beginning his long, adventurous life.

10

ANOTHER VERSION OF LIFE AND DEATH

There is a school of historians that believes reports of Sacagawea's death in 1812 were greatly exaggerated and that, in fact, she lived to a great old age, dying in 1884 at ninety-six or so on the Wind River Shoshone reservation in Wyoming. And, this school holds, Jean Baptiste lived there, too, and died there a year after his mother. He now has a marker next to what is said to be her grave.

This school was led by Grace Raymond Hebard, author of *Sacajawea, A guide and interpreter of the Lewis and Clark expedition*, published in 1933, and has been supported by a few other historians, although none recently.

Hebard was a professor of political economy at the University of Wyoming who consructed an elaborate tale of Sacajawea (she was consistent in her spelling of the Indian woman's name in that fashion, which was prior to the now accepted Sacagawea) on both the expedition and after. In 1902, Eva Emery Dye's book *The Conquest,* in effect discovered Sacagawea, whose role in the expedition hadn't been widely remarked at that point. Dye portrayed the Indian woman as a heroine who was largely responsible for the success of the mission. Hebard's book then raised her to near-sainthood—and extended her life.

Dye's book is a remarkable combination of diligent research and highly imaginative reconstruction of events of which there is no possibility of her having knowledge. For instance, the Oregon City, Oregon, author actually read the manuscript of Reuben G. Thwaites's authoritative edition of the Lewis and Clark Journals before it was published and, as a result, her recounting of those entries recorded in the journals is reliable.

But when she went beyond the record to construct dialogue supposedly spoken by the participants the book is, to put it charitably, creative.

Take, for example, the famous scene at Fort Clatsop where the captains have learned there is a whale on the beach miles south of them, near what is now Cannon Beach, Oregon. Clark made up a party; Sacagawea wasn't included. But she wanted to go.

So, Dye said, she slipped over to Clark, and said, "Captinne, you remember w'en we reach de rivers, and you knew not which to follow? I show de country an point de stream. Again w'en my husband could not spik, I spik for you.

"Now, Captinne, I travel great way to see de Beeg Water. I climb de mountain an' help de boat on de rapide. An' now dis monstous fish haf come." She could scarecely restrain her tears, Dye reported, and of course, Clark permitted her to go.

That speech is improbable in more ways than one. Sacagawea couldn't speak English, particularly English that seems to have been influenced by minstrel shows.

Hebard devoted most of her book to making the case that Sacagawea lived to a ripe old age. She said that Toussaint Charbonneau, working as a guide and interpreter at posts on the plains around 1820, and already equipped with two wives, Sacajawea and a new one, Eagle, took still another, a beautiful young Ute. She and senior wife Sacajawea got into a dispute and Charbonneau whipped the latter as a result.

So, Hebard reported, Sacajawea "disappeared from her tepee and left Charbonneau, never to return."

Presumably, Toussaint was comforted by his two remaining wives.

In this version, Sacajawea wandered for some time, making her home for a while with the Comanches in Oklahoma and eventually married one, infelicitously named Jerk Meat. By him she had five children, only two of whom survived and after Jerk Meat was killed in battle, she headed north, stopping en route to, perhaps, marry a Mexican soldier.

In 1843, John C. Fremont, on his second expedition to the west, recorded, in highly poetic fashion, that a French engage had been killed and while Fremont was camped at Fort St. Vrain, "The wife of the murdered man, an Indian woman of the Snake nation, desirous, like Naomi of old, to return to her people, requested and obtained permission to travel with my party to the neighborhood of Bear river, where she expected to meet with some of their villages. Happier than a Jewish widow, she carried with her two children, pretty little half-breeds, who added much to the liveliness of the camp. Her baggage was carried on five or six pack horses; and I gave her a small tent..." The woman traveled with Fremont for about three weeks and then left near Fort Bridger, "expecting to find some of her relations."

Hebard, from this slim evidence, concluded that this reference "in all probability refers to Sacajawea," and that "It was not at all strange that Sacajawea should have adopted the child of a French engage, even though the child might not have been her own;" Indians did that sort of thing. Besides, maybe she married the Frenchman.

Sacajawea also lived for a while near Virginia City, Montana, where, according to one of Professor Hebard's sources, "The white people had great admiration for her and did not require her to pay for anything she desired at the store;" she even was given a pass for the stage coaches along with orders to let her eat without charge at the stations. And she spent time with the Bannock Indians at Fort Hall.

But it was at Fort Bridger, the trading post and fort built in 1843 by the great mountain man Jim Bridger in the valley of the Green River to supply immigrants headed for Oregon and California that she was reunited with her wandering son Baptiste. Also there was an Indian man named Bazil, the son of her dead sister, whom she had last seen in 1805 during the expedition and whom she had adopted. Eventually Sacagawea wound up with her Shoshone tribe in the Wind River country, part of which became a reservation in 1868, and in 1871 she moved onto the reservation.

Along with Baptiste and his three wives and Basil and his three wives.

There the extended family lived happily. Sacagawea was an honored member of the tribe, sometimes known as Porivo, also as Lost Woman (from having disappeared from her Comanche friends after Jerk Meat's death and leaving behind, maybe, a son) and as Grass Maiden, Grass Woman and even Water-White-Man.

Then she died, in 1884, age about ninety-six, and was buried on the reservation, with only a small wooden slab to mark the spot. A year later, Baptiste died; he would have been eighty years old. His body was carried into the mountains and let down into a gully between two large boulders. Rocks then were thrown upon his body. A year later, 1886, Bazil died. His body was taken to a stream called Mill creek and placed in a cavern that was dug into the bank, which collapsed and buried his body.

In 1924—thirty-eight years after Bazil was buried in the cavern—his son located his grave and in 1925 Basil's bones were reburied, alongside Sacagawea.

A search for Baptiste's body was unsuccessful; a landslide had eliminated all evidence of the site.

This is the story told by Dr. Hebard, based upon interviews with elderly Indians, some of them one hundred years old, and white missonaries, Indian agents and teachers who had lived on the Wind River reservation.

And, importantly, by Dr. Charles A. Eastman. Dr. Eastman, a Sioux, a graduate of Dartmouth College and the School of Medicine of Boston University and the author of nine books about Indians, was asked by the Commissioner of the Bureau of Indian Affairs in 1925 to determine where Sacagawea was buried. One of his principal sources was a Mrs. Weidemann, who was eighty years old. She was the daughter of a chief named Poor Wolf, who was eight or nine years old when the Lewis and Clark expedition spent the winter of 1804-05 near his Hidatsa tribe. She related to Eastman the stories her father told her about Sacagawea then and later; the latter were based upon stories told to her father by a Hidatsa woman named Eagle, who supposedly was the wife of Toussaint Charbonneau when he married the beautiful Ute girl.

Based in part upon Eagle's stories as told to Poor Wolf and then related by Mrs. Weidemann many years later to Dr. Eastman, he decided that the Indian woman who had died at Fort Mandan in 1812 was not Sacagawea but another Shoshone wife of Charbonneau, named Otter Woman. And, he concluded, the Shoshone woman who died on the Wind River Reservation in 1884, was Sacagawea.

Dr. Eastman, in his report to the Commissioner of Indian Affairs in 1925 wrote:

"I submit the testimonies of three different nations, namely Shoshone, Comanches, and Gros Ventres, the first in Wyoming, the second in Oklahoma and the third in North Dakota. As there were no authentic records to be found after

Clark finished them, Bird Woman and sons, we have to accept the tribal traditions, and when they corroborate so strikingly well, we must accept as the truth.

" I report that Sacajawea, after sixty years of wandering from her own tribe, returned to her people at Fort Bridger and lived the remainder of her life with her sons in peace until she died April 9, 1884, at Fort Washakie, Wyoming. That is her final resting place."

In 1941 the Wyoming Historical Landmark Commission erected a monument to the Indian woman on Highway 287, two miles east of her grave site. In 1963 the Wyoming State Organization of the Daughters of the American Revolution erected a monument to her memory at the grave.

However, not everyone has accepted Dr. Eastman's "truth," this writer included.

Donald Jackson, editor of *Letters of the Lewis & Clark Expedition*, published by the University of Illinois Press, commented at length about the date of Sacagawea's death. He cited a cash book and journal kept by William Clark for the years 1825-1828 that wasn't found until 1955. The cover lists Clark's knowledge of the expedition members' whereabouts at that time.

Among the twenty-four entries on the roster:

Tous. Charbon Mand

Se car ja we au Dead

Tousant Charbon in Wertenburgh, Gy.

"Charbon" obviously refers to the Charbonneaus, father and son, with "Mand" refering to the former being at the Mandan villages. (And Clark's listing of "Tousant Charbon in Wertenburgh, Gy.," clears up another point of contention. Prince Paul's journal makes certain that it was Jean Baptiste Charbonneau whom he took to Germany. And Clark obviously knew the half-Indian youth's correct name—but referred to him in this instance by his father's name, a common practice those days.

In short, Clark's entry should have ended the speculation that Jean Baptiste had a brother named Toussaint.)

Says Jackson: "Surely Clark was the only person who could have drawn up such a roster at this time and included the present status of the expedition members; yet the roster is only as reliable as Clark's information. He is incorrect, for example in listing [Patrick] Gass as dead. We may expect him to have the most reliable information about those members of the party who were still in the West.

"The notation that Sacagawea was dead by 1825-28 is the most interesting piece of intelligence that Clark presents here, because it tends to contradict a popular belief. Sacagawea was never acclaimed as a real heroine by the American public until she was, in a sense, rediscovered by Eva Emery Dye in 1902. Then the task of elevating her to an even loftier position in history was assumed by Grace Raymond Hebard, who wrote *Sacajawea, a guide and interpreter of the Lewis and Clark expedition, with an account of the travels of Toussaint Charbonneau and of Jean Baptiste, the expedition papoose* (Glendale, Calif., 1933). Mrs. Hebard believed that Sacagawea had survived the rigors of her youth and was the very old Shoshoni woman of the same name who lived, until late in the ninteenth century, in the Wind River country of Wyoming. Other historians are inclined to suspect that Sacagawea may have died on the upper Missouri in 1812, in view of trader John Luttig's journal entry."

That entry, cited earlier, commented, without much punctuation, along with observations about the weather and the hunting, that "this evening the Wife of Charbonneau, a Snake Squaw, died of a putrid fever she was a good and the best Woman in the fort, aged abt 25 years she left a fine infant girl."

Jackson continued: "But, since Charbonneau had at least two wives, both Shoshoni, the matter has remained in doubt…

"Although Clark's notation here is not conclusive, it cannot be dismissed lightly. We are hardly justified in saying 'If Clark is wrong about Gass, then perhaps he is wrong about Sacagawea,' for the cases are different. Gass had gone back to Virginia and severed his contacts with the West, but Sacagawea, her husband Charbonneau, and her children were Clark's concern for many years after the expedition. He cared about them and felt a kind of responsibility for them. It is difficult to believe he could have been wrong about Sacagawea's death."

Harold P. Howard, in his 1971 book *Sacajawea*, published by the University of Oklahoma Press, pointed out that in 1884 the Reverand John Roberts, a missionary who had been on the Shoshone reservation in Wyoming for a year, officiated at the funeral of the woman he later identified as "Sacajawea of the Shoshonis." But, said Howard, at the time of her death Roberts evidently did not know that she was reputed to be the Sacajawea of the famous expedition. "The official form he completed at the time of her death states only that she was 'Bazil's mother.' Only later did Mr. Roberts comment on her supposed identity..."

Howard concluded, "It appears certain that an estimable Shonshoni woman lies buried on the Wind River Reservation, with a son on each side of her. It is equally certain, however, no written evidence or surviving objects prove that she was Sacajawea of the Lewis and Clark expedition."

In 1950, Russell Reid, the retired superintendent of the State Historical Society of North Dakota, wrote a booklet entitled *Sakakawea, The Bird Woman*. A longtime student of the expedition, Reid set out to refute the Hebard argument that the Indian woman lived until 1884.

Reid built his case upon entries in two different journals. One is by Henry Brackenridge, the writer and explorer quoted earlier, who on April 2, 1811, recorded that on the keelboat headed upriver to the Mandan and Hidatsa villages was Charbonneau and his wife of the Snake nation, "both of whom had accompanied

Lewis and Clark to the Pacific." He noted that the Indian woman "had becomed sickly."

That entry, coupled with that of Luttig's recording the death of "the Wife of Charbonneau, a Snake Squaw," in 1812, should put quits to the argument, Reid said, since the two prove that it was Sacagawea (or Sakakawea, in Reid's usage) who went up the river in 1811 and died there in 1812. And he made another point: "While the evidence given by Brackenridge and Luttig may be considered conclusive, the definite lack of evidence to support the Wyoming theory should be mentioned. After the Lewis and Clark expedition many traders, travelers and explorers visited the west. These men have left many fine journals in which they describe the history of the area, the Indians and trappers and points of interest. In these journals we find mention of Charbonneau and his son Baptiste, in fact in some of these instances we have good accounts of them. However, in spite of the fact that diligent search has been made by students in history no mention of Sakakawea has been found, after the statement of Luttig in 1812. If she had lived until 1884 surely some mention of her would have been made. From the records left by Lewis and Clark and Brackenridge we know that Sakakawea was an amiable and happy person, greatly attached to whites and for this reason her presence and her story would have been well known due to the fact that the area in which she was supposed to have lived was visited by white people for many years."

Reid added: "According to the testimony given by Dr. Roberts and others the Shoshone woman known by several other names before an effort was made to identify her as Sacajawea lived with two sons, Bazil and Baptiste....The son Baptiste is described as a man who took little interest in the affairs of his people and did not act as an interpreter or leader of his people. Dr. Roberts states that he knew little English. How could such a man be identified as the son of Sakakawea who was educated by Captain Clark and who later traveled extensively in Europe as the companion of Prince Paul Wilhelm, Duke of Wurtemburg? We have every reason to believe Baptiste Charbonneau received an education superior to that available to the average white man. On the frontier such an educational background would have clearly marked him as an outstanding individual. It was not until about 25 years later that a serious attempt was made to identify the old Shoshone woman as Sakakawea. In order to support this theory much evidence has been collected in the form of interviews, statements and affidavits. Most certainly no one has a right to question the motive nor honesty of individuals who gave such testimony but it should be pointed out that evidence of this kind is not always reliable. Far too often individuals are apt to confuse fact with fiction and stories that they have heard with some of their own experiences. For instance Bull's Eye, a reliable Hidatsa Indian, firmly believed and presented evidence to Dr. Eastman to convince him that Sakakawea was not a Shoshone at all but a Hidatsa."

The danger in relying upon the memories of elderly people is obvious, as Mr. Reid emphasized. Dr. Hebard in her book said that Mrs. Dye wrote her in 1906 that she had interviewed William Clark Kennerly, William Clark's nephew, in 1902. Hebard says Kennerly told Mrs. Dye he had known Baptiste Charbonneau "as a boy at school in St. Louis." Kennerly was seventy-eight when he was interviewed and he was remembering something that couldn't have happened. He wasn't born until four years after Baptiste left school in St. Louis.

And Bull's Eye, who claimed to be a grandson of Sacagawea, said she was killed by Indians near Glascow, Montana, in 1869.

Case settled? Probably not. But it should be.

Among his last acts in office in January, 2001, President Clinton did three things that relate to matters in this book.

One of them was to declare Pompey's Pillar a National Monument. The site, fifty-one acres along the Yellowstone River, is twenty-eight miles east of Billings, Montana. William Clark carved his name and the date—July 25, 1806—on the sandstone monolith, which has weathered to one hundred fifty feet from the two hundred feet it was when the expedition passed it returning to St. Louis. They can be seen today. "Pompey's Pillar is like a sandstone history book," the White House said.

The President also promoted William Clark to Captain, nearly two hundred years after that promotion was denied him by a bureaucratic War Department. No back pay was included.

"Unfortunately, issues of budget and bureaucracy intervened—some things never change—and Clark never received his commission," President Clinton said at a White House ceremony. "Today we honor his service."

The President presented a plaque to two of Clark's great-great-great-grandsons. The bill that led to the promotion stated that Clark "shall be deemed for all purposes to have held the grade of captain, rather than lieutenant, in the Regular Army, effective as of March 26, 1804, and continuing until his separation from the Army on February 17, 1807."

The ceremony was held in the East Room of the White House, where President Thomas Jefferson and Meriwether Lewis planned the Lewis and Clark Expedition.

Finally, Clinton awarded Sacagawea and York, Clark's slave, with the titles of Honorary Sergeant in the Army.

The Indian woman and the black man were the only members of the expedition who weren't paid for their services.

Except, of course, for Jean Baptiste Charbonneau.

11

EPILOGUE

William Bent was one of four brothers, all of whom were in the fur trade. William was trapping on the upper Arkansas as early as 1824. He became a partner with his brother Charles and Ceran St. Vrain; the latter two had built what became known as Bent's Fort, a huge adobe structure, largest fort in the Southwest, on the Arkansas river in 1833 for the Indian trade. William became its manager. The army made extensive use of the fort as a staging area for its operations in the Southwest and in 1846 he, along with Tom Fitzpatrick, guided Stephen Watts Kearny's troops from the fort to Santa Fe. Disgusted at the low price the army offered to pay for the fort, he blew it up. He later built another, thirty-eight miles downstream, known as Bent's New Fort, which eventually was rented to the army. But the army stopped paying the rent after a year and Bent spent years traveling to Washington trying to collect; it was never settled. William Bent admired most Indians and tried, along with Kit Carson, to arrange peaceful accommodation between them and whites in the southwest, but with little success. In 1869, leading a caravan from Santa Fe to his ranch on the Purgatoire River, he developed pneumonia and died there May

19. He was nearly sixty. His brother Charles, who had been appointed governor of New Mexico, was murdered in Taos in 1847 by Indians and Mexicans rebelling against the American occupation.

Jim Bridger, mountain man and Indian fighter, spent most of his life after his fur-trading days as a guide and scout. His famed knowledge of the West—he probably was the first white man to see the Great Salt Lake—led to his hiring for at least a dozen expeditions in the mountain West. Historian Bernard DeVoto called him "an atlas of the West." His most famous job probably was the work he did for General Grenville Dodge in mapping the route for the Union Pacific Railroad. In 1881 "Old Gabe," suffering from years of poor health and nearly blind, died on his farm near Little Santa Fe, Missouri, and was buried near by. He was seventy seven. In 1904 General Dodge, always a great admirer of Bridger, arranged for the reburying of his remains in Mt. Washington Cemetery, Independence, Missouri. A seven-foot monument stands at the head of his grave.

Christopher "Kit" Carson, famed as a scout and indian fighter, spent the years 1842 to 1847 as a scout and guide for the expeditions of John C. Fremont. When the hostilities in California ended, he tried to take up ranching near Taos but for most of the rest of his life he served with the military. He was a scout in Apache country, and reentering the army as a colonel of the First New Mexico Volunteer Regiment, saw action in the Battle of Valverde on the Rio Grande and was promoted to brigadier general. After a scorched-earth war against the Navajos in New Mexico and Arizona, he forced the surrender and internment of eight thousand Navajos. His last Indian campaign was in 1864 when he led an expedition against Kiowas and Comanches in the Texas Panhandle. After the Indian wars, Carson took command of Fort Garland, Colorado Territory, as a colonel of the regular army. He was discharged in 1867. Then the old Indian fighter ended his career—as Superintendent of Indian Affairs for Colorado Territory. As such he led a delegation of Utes to Washington to lobby for a treaty guaranteeing them hunting rights. But his health had been deteriorating for years, and on May 23, 1868 he died of an aneurism at Fort Lyon. He was sixty years old. He was buried in Boggsville, Colorado, but in 1869 his remains and those of his wife, who had died a month earlier, were reburied in Taos.

William Clark spent most of his life after the Lewis and Clark Expedition involved in Indian affairs, but one of his tasks was to arrange publication of the expedition journals. Meriwether Lewis was supposed to have done that but died in mysterious circumstances. As reward for his role in the expedition, President Jefferson appointed Clark Indian agent for the Louisiana Territory. In 1813, he became governor of Missouri Territory—previously called Louisiana Territory— built Fort Osage and worked to maintain friendly relations with the tribes of the Missouri and upper Mississippi. Tribes frequently visited his farm for parleys. In 1820 Clark was defeated in his bid to become the first governor of Missouri after statehood, but continued in charge of Indian matters and in 1822, in a newly created position, became Superintendent of Indian Affairs, at St. Louis. He mainly was involved with the removal of Indians living east of the Mississippi and in Missouri to lands in eastern Kansas. He died in St. Louis, age sixty eight, in 1838.

Phillip St. George Cooke, under the command of General Stephen Watts Kearny, conducted Captain John C. Fremont from California to Washington where both testified against Fremont at his court martial for refusing to obey Kearny, his superior officer in California. He then became superintendent of Carlisle Barracks, commanded the Second Dragoons in Texas, fought the Souix and served in Kansas during the anti-slavery uprising there. He commanded the calvary in the so-called Utah War of 1857, when Brigham Young resisted the federal government's authority. During the Civil War he served as a Union cavalry officer and was promoted to major general in 1865 for his service. He retired in 1873 and wrote *Conquest of New Mexico and California* before his death in Detroit at age eighty six in 1895.

Thomas Fitzpatrick, known as "Broken Hand" because of injuries he had suffered when a rifle blew up in his hands, had three careers—fur trapper and trader, guide and Indian agent. As a trapper and trader he ranged the west as far as Oregon, and ran the Rocky Mountain Fur Company, which he purchased with his friend Jim Bridger, Milton Sublette and two others. The fur trade dying, he became a guide for a long list of notables. He led the first emigrant wagon train to Oregon and California, was guide for Captain John C. Fremont on his second, and longest, to Oregon and then California, was a guide for General Stephen Watts Kearny twice on military expeditions, including the one during the Mexican War when he took the troops to Santa Fe. Sent with dispatches back to Washington, while there he was appointed Indian agent for the Upper Platte and Arkansas. He worked for years to bring peace between the warring Plains tribes, holding famous conferences in 1851 and 1853 to mark tribal boundaries and make treaties. In 1854 he went to Washington to see that the treaties were approved. But he got pneumonia there and died February 7, 1854, in a Washington hotel, and was buried in the Congressional Cemetery. He was fifty five.

John C. Fremont was found guilty on three counts of mutiny, disobedience and conduct prejudicial to military discipline in his court martial in 1848 in Washington after being returned there under guard. Because the judges recommended clemency President James Polk ordered him returned to duty but Fremont resigned the army instead. That winter he took his fourth expedition west into southern Colorado, which was a disaster. Ten of his men died in a snowstorm. In 1853 he made another expedition of the west, his fifth, crossing the San Juan mountains in winter. When gold was found on land he had purchased near Yosmite Valley, he became a millionaire and served a year as one of California's first senators. He gave up that position to return to his mines. In 1856 he was the nominee for president of the new Republican party but lost to James Buchanan in a vicious campaign. During the Civil War he was made a major general and sent to St. Louis but was dismissed by President Abraham Lincoln after one hundred days after he issued his own emancipation proclamation. In 1864 he was endorsed as a candidate for president by the radical wing of the Republican party but withdrew before the election. He lost his California lands, and his fortune, in railroad speculations. He was appointed territorial governor of Arizona as the result of his service to the Republican Party and served three years. In 1890, almost penniless, Congress granted him a pension of six thousand dollars a year. But he died in July of that year in a New York City hotel of a burst appendix. He was seventy seven.

Stephen Watts Kearny, after testifying against John C. Fremont at his court martial, joined General Winfield Scott's army of occupation in Mexico and served briefly as military commander at Vera Cruz. He contracted yellow fever and came home in July 1848. When he was nominated for promotion to major general for "gallant conduct at San Pascual and for meritorious conduct in California and New Mexico," Senator Thomas Hart Benton, Fremont's father-in-law, filibustered for thirteen days in the Senate against the promotion—to no avail. Kearny died in St. Louis from the effects of the fever, in October, 1848. He was fifty four years old.

Zenas Leonard retired from the fur trade in 1835 after traveling with Joseph Walker's brigade to California via the Humboldt River. He became a retailer, Indian trader and steamboat operator in Sibley, Missouri. He died at age forty eight. His memoir, *Narrative of Zenas Leonard,* is one of the classic accounts of the fur trade.

Meriwether Lewis was appointed governor of Louisiana Territory by President Jefferson after his return from the Pacific, but served less than two years. In 1809 he left St. Louis for Washington to defend himself against criticism of his governorship and to arrange publication of the journals of the expedition, which he had kept putting off. En route he stopped overnight at a tavern on the Natchez Trace seventy miles southwest of Nashville and died there the next morning, October 11, of two gunshot wounds, leaving one of the enduring mysteries of American history: Suicide or murder?

Prince Paul Friedrich Wilhelm, Duke of Wurttemberg, who had taken Baptiste to Europe, returned to his palace at Mergentheim, Germany, in 1856 after his fifth trip to America. He died there in 1860, age sixty three. Later his son sold Prince Paul's scientific collection, books, manuscripts and notes and most of them were lost to posterity. There is a legend that an illegitimate daughter named Pauline, mother unidentified, followed Prince Paul to America, eventually married and had a family, and that some descendants still live in Missouri.

James K. Polk, eleventh president of the United States, came to office in 1845 intending to annex Texas, acquire California—California in those days included the present states of California, New Mexico, Nevada, Utah, Arizona and parts of Wyoming, Idaho and Colorado—and settle the Oregon boundary question with

Great Britain. In his single term of office he did all three, adding more than five hundred thousand square miles to the United States. Harry S. Truman called him a great president: "said what he intended to do and did it." Three months after voluntarily leaving office in 1849, he died at Nashville, Tennessee, age fifty three, having completed the expansion of the United States started by Thomas Jefferson with the Lewis and Clark Expedition.

Osborne Russell worked as a trapper for Nathaniel Wyeth and was in charge of Fort Hall, the trading post built by Wyeth on the Snake River, during the winter of 1834-35. He then went to work for the Rocky Mountain Fur Company and later the American Fur Company. In 1842 Russell joined a wagon train and traveled to Oregon, where he trained himself to be a lawyer and was appointed judge by the provisional government. When Oregon became a territory in 1848, Russell was elected to the legislature. But he was struck by California's gold fever that year and traveled to the gold fields there, where he was drafted as a judge for the vigilante trials held in Placerville. He lived the rest of his life there as a miner and businessman, dying in 1892 at age seventy eight.

Sir William Drummond Stewart, the Scottish ex-army captain who made two tours of the American West, traveling as far as Fort Vancouver on the Columbia River, continued his traveling after he returned home, roaming the continent and going as far as Russia. His son George was a member of the famous Light Brigade that made the charge during the Crimean War, and won the Victoria Cross for his gallantry. Sir William died in 1871 at age seventy seven at his Scottish castle, Murthly.

William Sublette was the oldest of five brothers, all of whom worked the fur trade, Milton being the most well known. William spent from 1823 until 1836 in the mountains as a trader and trapper; he was wounded in the famous Battle of Pierre's Hole of 1832 by the Blackfeet. In 1836 he left the mountains for St. Louis to become a supplier of goods for the fur trade, a farmer; he also entered a variety of other businesses. He had three coal mines, raised pedigree cattle imported from England, served as a bank director and helped found an insurance company. He built a resort on his farm at Sulphur Springs, Missouri, near St. Louis, and added a race track.He also was active in Democratic politics but was defeated in his campaign for a seat in the Missouri state senate. In 1845, newly married, he and his wife started for Cape May, New Jersey, to spend the summer. But he became ill en route and died of tuberculosis in a Pittsburg hotel. He was forty-six. He originally was buried on his farm but several years later his remains were reburied in Bellefontaine Cemetery, St. Louis.

John A. Sutter, "the King of California," was ruined by the discovery of gold on his land.The gold rush brought thousands of men who overran his property, destroyed his fields and slaughtered his herds. By 1852 he was bankrupt. He was granted a pension by the California legislature—he'd been a delegate to the convention that drafted California's constitution—moved to Lancaster County, Pennslyvania and spent the rest of his life petitioning the government for compensation for the loss of his California lands; the Supreme Court eventually disallowed the claims. He died in 1880 at age 77.

Nathaniel Wyeth failed in the fur trade despite his best efforts over a five-year period. He planned his first expedition west in two parts. He would meet the ship Sultana, which was to sail to the Columbia River around Cape Horn while he led a party overland, hunting and trapping on the way. Reaching the Columbia he'd load his cargo of furs aboard, and return to Boston to sell them. But his expedition ran into trouble; trapping was poor, seven men deserted, and when he finally reached the Columbia he learned the ship had been wrecked in the South Pacific. So he headed home overland but not before making a deal with Milton Sublette and Thomas Fitzpatrick to supply them with goods he planned bringing back in 1834. In Boston he refinanced and chartered a ship, the May Dacre, which was to sail to the Columbia where it would be loaded with salmon to take back to Boston. But on his trip overland with his goods, Sublette and Fitzpatrick refused to honor the deal. Stuck with the goods, he moved on to the Snake River, where he built Fort Hall, planning to trade for furs. Leaving Osborne Russell in charge there, he moved on to the Columbia again where he found that his ship had been damaged by lightening and arrived too late for the salmon run. He sent it to Hawaii with a load of timber, and the next year tried again. But he still was unable to get a full cargo of fish, gave up and returned home, selling Fort Hall to the Hudson's Bay Company. In New England, he returned to the ice business which he'd left for his adventures in the west, and by 1848 sixty thousand tons of ice were being shipped each year to the southern states, the Caribbbean and at least once as far as Calcutta. He died in Cambridge, Massachusetts, in 1856 at age fifty four, a wealthy man.

BIBLIOGRAPHY

Abert, James William. Expedition to the Southwest—An 1845 Reconnaissance of Colorado, New Mexico, Texas and Oklahoma. *University of Nebraska Press, Lincoln, Bison Books edition, 1999.*

Alter, J. Cecil. Jim Bridger. *University of Oklahoma Press, Norman. 1962.*

Ambrose, Stephen E. Undaunted Courage—Meriwether Lewis, Thomas Jefferson, and the Opening of the American West. *Simon & Schuster, New York, 1996.*

American Fur Company Account Books 1840-43. *Missouri Historical Society, St. Louis.*

Anderson, Irving W. A Charbonneau Family Portrait. *Fort Clatsop Historical Association, Astoria, Oreg., 1992..*

——Sacajawea?—Sakakawea?—Sacagawea? *We Proceeded On, pub. of Lewis and Clark Trail Heritage Foundation, Great Falls, Mont., Summer, 1975.*

Anderson, William Marshall. Rocky Mountain Journals. Edited by Dale L. Morgan and Eleanor Towles Harris. *University of Nebraska Press, Lincoln,, Bison Books edition, 1987. Reprint.*

Angel, Myron. History of Placer County, California. *Thompson & West, Oakland, Cal., 1882.*

Bakeless, John. Lewis and Clark, Partners in Discovery. *William Morrow & Co., New York, 1947.*

Bancroft, Hubert Hugh. History of California, Vols 1-7, pub. 1884 through 1890. *A.L. Bancroft & Co., San Francisco; Bancroft & Co., San Francisco; Arno Press, New York..*

Beckwourth, James P. The Life and Adventures of James P. Beckwourth, as told to Thomas D. Bonner. *University of Nebraska Press, Lincoln, Bison Book edition, 1981.Reprint.*

Berry, Don. A Majority of Scoundrels. *Ballantine Books, New York, 1971.*

Biddle, Nicholas. History of the Expedition under the Command of Captains Lewis and Clark. 3 vols. *New Amsterdam Book Company, New York, 1902. Reprint.*

Brackenridge, Henry M. Journal of a Voyage up the Missouri. *Pub. in vol. 6, Early Western Travels, Reuben G. Thwaites, ed.. A.H. Clark, Cleveland, 1904.*

Carson, Kit (Christopher). Kit Carson's Autobiography. Milo M. Quaife, ed. *University of Nebraska Press, Lincoln, Bison Book edition, 1966.*

Charbonneau, Jean Baptiste. Letters to a judge while Alcalde of San Luis Rey, 1849. *Brigham Young University Library Special Collections, Provo, Utah.*

Chardon, F. A. Chardon's Journal At Fort Clark, 1834-1839. Annie Heloise Abel, ed. *University of Nebraska Press, Lincoln, Bison Book edition, 1997.*

Carter, Harvey L. "William H. Ashley." Mountain Men & Fur Traders of the Far West, LeRoy Hafen, ed. *University of Nebraska Press, Lincoln, Bison Book edition, 1982.*

Catlin, George. Letters and Notes on the North American Indians. Michael Macdonald, ed. *C.N. Potter, New York, 1975.*

Chittenden, Hiram M. The American Fur Trade of the Far West. 2 vols. *University of Nebraska Press, Lincoln, 1986. Reprint.*

Chuinard, E.G. Only One Man Died: The Medical Aspects of the Lewis and Clark Expedition. *Arthur H. Clark Co., Glendale, Cal., 1979.*

Clark, Ella E. and Edmonds, Margot. Sacagawea of the Lewis & Clark Expedition. *University of California Press, Berkeley & Los Angeles, 1979.*

Clark, William. Account Book, May 25, 1825, to June 14, 1828. *The Newberry Library, Special Collections, Chicago.*

Cleland, Robert Glass. This Reckless Breed of Men. *Alfred A. Knopf, New York, 1963.*

Clyman, James. Journal of a Mountain Man. Linda M. Hasselstrom, ed.*Mountain Press Publishing Co., Missoula, Mont., 1984.*

Cooke, Philip St. George. The Conquest of New Mexico and California. *G.P. Putnam's Sons, New York, 1878.*

Coues, Elliott, ed. The History of the Lewis and Clark Expedition.3 vols. *Dover Publications, Inc., New York, 1965. Reprint.*

Crawford, Helen. Sakakawea. *North Dakota Historical Society Quarterly, Bismarck, April, 1927.*

Cutright, Paul Russell. A History of the Lewis and Clark Journals. *University of Oklahoma Press, Norman, 1976.*

Dary, David. The Santa Fe Trail—Its History, Legends, and Lore. *Alfred A. Knopf, New York, 2000.*

DeVoto, Bernard. The Course of Empire.*Houghton Mifflin, Boston, 1952.*

————The Journals of Lewis and Clark. *Houghton Mifflin, Boston, 1953.*

————The Year of Decision—1846. *Houghton Mifflin, Boston, Sentry Edition, 1961.*

————Across the Wide Missouri. *Houghton Mifflin, Boston, 1947.*

Dye, Eva Emery. The Conquest. *A.C. McClurg, Chicago, 1903.*

————-Correspondence With Grace Raymond Hebard, 1906, 1907,1924. *Oregon Historical Society, Portland.*

Duncan, Dayton and Burns, Ken. Lewis & Clark—The Journey of the Corps of Discovery. *Alfred A. Knopf, Inc.,New York, 1997.*

Engelhardt, Father Zephyrin. San Luis Rey Mission, series, Missions and Missionaries of California. *James H. Barry Company, San Francisco, 1921.*

Farnham, Thomas Jefferson. Farnham's Travels. *Early Western Travels, Reuben Gold Thwaites, ed., vol. 28. A. H. Clark, Cleveland, 1906.*

Ferris, Warren A. Life in the Rocky Mountains. *The Old West Publishing Co., Denver, 1983. Reprint.*

Field, Matthew C. Prairie and Mountain Sketches.Kate L.Gregg and John F. McDermott, eds. *University of Oklahoma Press, Norman, 1957.*

Fremont, John Charles. A Report on An Exploration of the Country Lying Between the Missouri River and the Rocky Mountains, on the line of the Kansas and Great Platte Rivers. *Ye Galleon Press, Fairfield, Wash., 1996. Reprint.*

————-Memoirs of My Life. Only one vol. published. *Belford Clarke & Co., Chicago, 1887.*

Furtwangler, Albert. Sacagawea's Son as a Symbol. *Oregon Historical Quarterly, Fall 2001, Portland.*

————-Sacagawea's Son. New Evidence from Germany. *Oregon Historical Quarterly, Winter, 2002, Portland.*

Gass, Patrick. A Journal of the Voyages and Travels of a Corps of Discovery under the command of Captain Lewis and Captain Clark. *Ross and Haines, Minneapolis, 1958. Reprint.*

Garst, Shannon. Broken-Hand Fitzpatrick, Greatest of Mountain Men. *J. Messner, New York, 1961.*

Gilbert. Bil. Westering Man - The Life of Joseph Walker. *Athenium, New York, 1983.*

Guild, Thelma S., and Carter, Harvey L. Kit Carson—A Pattern for Heroes. *University of Nebraska Press, Lincoln, Bison Book, 1988.*

Hafen, Ann W. "Jean Baptiste Charbonneau." LeRoy Hafen, The Mountain Men and the Fur Trade of the Far West. *Arthur H. Clark Co., Glendale, Cal., 1972.*

Hafen, LeRoy, ed. Trappers of the Far West. *Arthur H. Clark Co., Glendale, Cal.,1965.*

———Broken Hand, the life of Thomas Fitzpatrick. *University of Nebraska Press. Lincoln, Bison Book edition, 1981.*

———Mountain Men & Fur Trade of the Far West. *University of Nebraska Press, Lincoln, Bison Book edition, 1982. Reprint.*

———The W.M. Boggs Manuscript About Bent's Fort, Kit Carson, the Far West and Life Among the Indians. *Colorado Magazine, Denver, March, 1930.*

Hebard, Grace Raymond. Sacajawea, A guide and interpreter of the Lewis and Clark expedition, with an account of the travels of Toussaint Charbonneau, and of Jean Baptiste, the expedition papoose. *Arthur H. Clark Company, Glendale, Calif., 1933.*

Howard, Harold P. Sacajawea. *University of Oklahoma Press, Norman, 1971.*

Howard, Helen. The Mystery of Sacajawea's Death. *Pacific Northwest Quarterly, pub. of Washington State Historical Society, Seattle, January, 1967.*

Irving, Washington. Adventures of Captain Bonneville.*Binfords & Mort, Portland, Or., 1954. Reprint.*

Jackson, Donald D., ed. Letters of the Lewis and Clark Expedition. 2 vols. *University of Illinois Press, Urbana and Chicago, 1978.*

Kennerly, William Clark. Persimmon Hill—A Narrative of Old St. Louis and the Far West, as told to Elizabeth Russell. *University of Oklahoma Press, Norman, 1948.*

Kingston, C.S. Sacagawea as Guide—The Evaluation of a Legend. *Pacific Northwest Quarterly, pub. of Washington State Historical Society, Seattle, January, 1944.*

Lavender, David. The Way to the Western Sea—Lewis and Clark Across the Continent.*Harper & Row, New York, 1988.*

———Bent's Fort. *University of Nebraska Press, Bison Book edition. Reprint, 1972.*

Large, Arlen J. Sacagawea Takes Her Place With the Goddess of Love and Beauty. *We Proceeded On, pub. of Lewis And Clark Trail Heritage Foundation, Great Falls, Mont., Nov. 1989.*

———Pompey's Pillar. *We Proceeded On, Aug. 1990.*

———The Clark-Sacagawea Affair: A literary evolution. *We Proceeded On, Aug. 1988.*

Larpenteur, Charles. Forty Years a Fur Trader. *Lakeside Press, Chicago, 1933.*

Leonard, Zenas. Adventures of a Mountain Man—the narrative of Zenas Leonard. *University of Nebraska Press, Lincoln, 1978.*

Lewis, Oscar. Sutter's Fort. *Prentice-Hall, Inc., Englewood Cliffs, N.J. 1966.*

Luttig, John C. Journal of a Fur-Trading Expedition on the Upper Missouri 1812-1813. Stella M. Drumm, ed. *Argosy-Antiquarian Ltd., New York, 1964. Reprint.*

McCracken, Harold. George Catlin and the Old Frontier. *Dial Press, New York, 1959.*

Moore, Bob. Pompey's Baptism. *We Proceeded On, pub. of Lewis And Clark Trail Heritage Foundation, Great Falls, Mont., Feb. 2000.*

Morgan, Dale L. Jedediah Smith and the Opening of the West.*Bobbs-Merrill, New York, 1953.*

————The West of William H. Ashley. *Old West Publishing Co., Denver, 1964.*

Moulton, Gary E. ed. Atlas of the Lewis and Clark Expedition. *University of Nebraska Press, 1981.*

Newell, Robert. Memoranda. Dorothy O. Johansen, ed.*Champoeg Press, Portland, Ore., 1959.*

Parkman, Frances. The California and Oregon Trail: Being Sketches of Prairie and Rocky Mountain Life. *George P. Putnam, New York, 1849.*

Porter, Clyde H. Jean Baptiste Charbonneau. *Idaho Yesterdays, pub. of Idaho State Historical Society, Boise, Fall, 1961.*

Porter, Mae Reed and Davenport, Odessa. Scotsman in Buckskin—Sir William Drummond Stewart and The Rocky Mountain Fur Trade. *Hastings House, New York, 1963.*

Reid, Russell. Sakakawea: The Bird Woman. *State Historical Society of North Dakota, Bismarck, 1986.*

Ricketts, Norma Baldwin. The Mormon Battalion. *Utah State University Press, Logan, 1996.*

Roberts. David. A Newer World. Kit Carson, John C. Fremont, and the Claiming of the American West. *Simon & Schuster, New York, Touchstone edition, 2001.*

Russell, Osborne. Journal of a Trapper. Aubrey L. Haines, ed. *MJF Books, New York, 1955.*

Ruxton, George Frederick. Adventures in Mexico and the Rocky Mountains. *Harper & Brothers, New York, 1848.*

————-In The Old West. *The Macmillan Company, New York, 1924.*

Sachsen-Altenburg, Hans von, and Dyer, Robert L. Duke Paul of Wuerttemberg on the Missouri Frontier: 1823, 1830 and 1851. *Pekitanoul Publications, Booneville, Mo., 1998.*

Sage, Rufus B. Rocky Mountain Life. *University of Nebraska Press, Lincoln, Bison Book edition, 1982. Reprint.*

Schultz, James Willard. Bird Woman: Sacagawea's Own Story.*Mountain Meadow Press, Missoula, Mont., 1999. Reprint.*

Smith, E. Willard. Journal of E. Willard Smith While With The Fur Traders Vasquez And Sublette, In The Rocky Mountain Region, 1839-1840. *Oregon Historical Society Quarterly, Portland, Vol. 14, No. 3.*

Samuels, Peggy and Harold. The Illustrated Biographical Encyclopedia of Artists of the American West. *Doubleday & Co., New York, 1976.*

Spence, Mary Lee and Jackson, Donald, eds. The Expeditions of John Charles Fremont. 2 vols. *University of Illinois Press, Chicago, 1937.*

Stegner, Wallace. Beyond the Hundredth Meridian. *Houghton Mifflin Co., Boston, 1954.*

Sublette, Solomon. Correspondence. *Sublette Papers, Missouri Historical Society, St. Louis, 1844.*

Thomas, George. Lewis and Clark Trail—The Photo Journal. *Pictorial Histories Publishing Co., Missoula, Mont., 2000.*

Thompson, Harry F. Meriwether Lewis and His Son: The Claim of Joseph DeSomet Lewis and the Problem of History. *North Dakota History, pub. of State Historical Society of North Dakota, Bismarck, Vol. 67, No.3, 2000.*

Thwaites, Reuben Gold, ed. The Original Journals of the Lewis and Clark Expedition. 8 vols. *Dodd, Mead & Co., New York, 1904.*

————Newly Discovered Personal Records of Lewis & Clark. *Shorey Book Store, Seattle, 1971. Facsimile of June, 1904, Scribner's Magazine.*

Tobie, Harvey E. "Joseph L.Meek." Pub. in Mountain Men & Fur Traders of the Far West, LeRoy R. Hafen, ed. *University of Nebraska Press, Lincoln, Bison Book edition, 1982.*

Tyler, Daniel. A Concise History of the Mormon Battalion in the Mexican War 1846- 1848. *Rio Grande Press, Glorieta, N.M., 1969. Reprint.*

Vestal, Stanley. Joe Meek—The Merry Mountain Man. *University of Nebraska Press, Lincoln, Bison Book, 1952.*

————Jim Bridger, Mountain Man. *William Morrow & Co., New York, 1946.*

————Kit Carson—The Happy Warrior of the Old West. *Houghton Mifflin Co., Boston, 1928.*

Victor, Francis Fuller. River of the West: The Adventures of Joe Meek. *Mountain Press Publishing Co., Missoula, Mont., 1985. Reprint.*

Walker, Dale L. Bear Flag Rising. The Conquest of California, 1846. *Forge, New York, 1999.*

————Pacific Destiny: The Three-Century Journey to the Oregon Country. *Forge, New York, 2000.*

Wheeler, Olin D. The Trail of Lewis and Clark, 1804-1904. 2 vols. *G.P. Putnam's Sons, New York, 1904.*

White, James Haley. St. Louis and Its Men Fifty Years Ago. *Missouri Historical Society, St. Louis, 1882.*

Wilhelm, Prince Paul, Duke of Wuerttemberg. First Journey to North America in the Years 1822 to 1824. Translated by William G. Bek. *State Historical Society, Pierre, S.D. 1941. Vol. 19, 1938.*

————A Brief Sketch of St. Louis in 1851.*Grace Raymond Hebard Papers, American Heritage Center, University of Wyoming, Laramie.*

——Notes on Meeting Baptiste Charbonneau, 1823. *Grace Raymond Hebard Papers, American Heritage Center, University of Wyoming, Laramie. Translated by Gene Wright, 2000.*

——Early Sacramento—Glimpses of John Augustus Sutter, The Hok Farm and the Neighboring Indian Tribes. *American Heritage Center, University of Wyoming,* Laramie, 1851. Translated by Louis C. Butscher.

Wishart, David J. The Fur Trade of the American West 1807-1840. *University of Nebraska Press, Lincoln, 1979.*

Work, John. Journal of John Work, 1830-1831. *Newberry Library, Chicago, 1905.*

Wyeth, John B. A Short History of a Long Journey. *Ye Galleon Press, Fairfield, Wash., 1970.*

Wyeth, Nathaniel J. The Correspondence and Journals of Captain Nathaniel J. Wyeth, 1831-1836. *University Press, Eugene, Or., 1899.*

Newspapers

Idaho Statesman, Boise, January 2, 1971. "Preservation Urged for Grave Location of Sacajawea's Son South of Jordan Valley."

Malheur Enterprise, Ontario, Oreg., July 28, 1971. "Gravesite to be dedicated Aug.6."

Owyhee Avalanche, Ruby City, Idaho, June 2, 1866.Obituary of "J. B. Charbouneau."

Ontario Argus Observer, Ontario, Oreg., February 10, 1966. "Sacajawea's Son's Long-Lost Grave May Be Rescued from Oblivion," by Chris Moore.

——December 17, 1970. "State Urges Clearing Title To Grave of Charbonneau."

The Placer Herald, Auburn, Cal., July 7, 1866."Death of a California Pioneer."

The Register-Guard, Eugene, Oreg., January 18, 2001. "William Clark promoted—200 years later." Associated Press.

The Sunday Oregonian, Portland, December 5, 1965. "The Unmarked Grave of Sacajawea's Son," by Christine Moore.

————June 25, 2000. "Paying tribute to expedition's 'Pomp,'" by Peter Sleeth.

————July 23, 2000. "Riding back on Sacagawea's legend.The Lemhi Shoshone hope to return to their homeland," by Peter Sleeth.

————January 21, 2001. "A monumental debate. A grain exporter wants to build four silos near Pompey's Pillar," by Peter Sleeth.

The World, Coos Bay, Oreg., May 3, 2000. "Grave of Sacagawea's Son getting spruced up for 2003." Associated Press.

ABOUT THE AUTHOR

Frederick Taylor, a native Oregonian, spent 30 years as a reporter and editor with The Wall Street Journal, the last 14 as managing editor and then executive editor. As a reporter he wrote many of the long, front-page stories that have made The Journal famous. For 10 years after his retirement there he published and edited a weekly newspaper in Coquille, Oregon. He became interested in Sacagawea's son, Jean Baptiste Charbonneau, when he discovered that, although Pomp lived a long, exciting life, he'd been only the subject of essays. Taylor thought he deserved more.

This book contains what he found.

Taylor lives with his wife, Georga, on the Southern Oregon coast.